Memorybot

For Rachel

Memorybot

AI and the End of Human Memory

ANDREW HOSKINS

polity

First published in 2026 by Polity Press Ltd.

Polity Press Ltd.
65 Bridge Street
Cambridge CB2 1UR, UK

Polity Press Ltd.
111 River Street
Hoboken, NJ 07030, USA

ISBN-13: 978-1-5095-7373-8
ISBN-13: 978-1-5095-7374-5(pb)

A catalogue record for this book is available from the British Library.

Library of Congress Control Number: 2026936872

Typeset in 11 on 14pt Warnock Pro
by Cheshire Typesetting Ltd, Cuddington, Cheshire
Printed and bound in Great Britain by Ashford Colour Ltd.

For further information on Polity, visit our website:
politybooks.com

Contents

Acknowledgements

I was originally inspired to read and think about memory by my first PhD supervisor, Deirdre Boden, in Sociology at Lancaster University in the mid-1990s. Since then, my own journey through the shifting technologies and media that constantly reshape memory has been influenced by many great colleagues and friends. I am indebted to William Merrin, still the most underrated and amazing media theorist of his generation, for his constant inspiration and support.

I am also very grateful to Mary Savigar at Polity for her faith and support in this project, and to the Polity Editorial Board and the anonymous reviewers of the drafts of my manuscript for their always constructive and enthusiastic feedback and advice.

I am also indebted to all those who have generously given their time to speak with me about their work as expert memory app and service designers, CEOs and journalists, including: Jacob Appel, Lauren Goode, Laura Guien, Suman Kanuganti, Sam Kececi, Cesar Kuriyama, Matt Raoul and Jonathan Wegener.

Many others have contributed to my thinking and writing on media and memory over the years, and I am very grateful to: Ben O'Loughlin, Kristína Čimová, Geoff Bowker, Amanda Barnier, Catherine Happer, Mark Neville, Andrea Luka Zimmerman, Shona Illingworth, Anthony Downey, Ryan Calo, John Tulloch, Gillian Youngs, Steve Brown, Paula Reavey, John Sutton, Katerina Linden, Qi Wang, Renata Salecl, Kate Wright, Danny Pilkington, Nuria Lorenzo-Dus and Sasha Kletsov.

I am particularly obliged to Luli van der Does, Director of the Center for Peace at Hiroshima University, for our collaboration over a decade and for enabling my engagement with the *Hibakusha*, the community of survivors of the atomic bombings of Japan, and to learn from them about the nature and importance of living memory at the end of a generation.

This work is also informed by generous engagement from audiences at talks I have given over the past three years, and I am very grateful for these opportunities and invitations from: Leighton Edwards (Swansea University), Avishek Parui and Merin Simi Raj (IIT Madras, Chennai), Catherine O'Leary (St Andrews), Armina Omerika (Goethe Universität, Frankfurt), Boris Noordenbos (Yerevan State University), Jamievee Bautista and Stefano Filippini (Scuola Normale Superiore, Florence), Tabea Widmann (Zeppelin Museum, Friedrichshafen), Gerd Debald, Oliver Dimbath, Nina Leonhard and Mathias Berek (TU, Berlin), Robin Ekelund (Malmö University), Jānis Karlsbergs and Elina Lange (NATO), Christine Lohmeier (University of Salzburg), Christian Pentzold (University of Leipzig) and the Hiroshima Peace Memorial Museum.

I am also very grateful to the students on my Media, AI and Memory course, whom I have the privilege to teach and learn from, and to my colleagues in the vibrant Department of Sociology at the University of Edinburgh.

Last and not least (but loudest), I am constantly inspired by my three children, Jasper, Atticus and Loretta, all remembering and forgetting in the era of generative artificial intelligence.

1

Your Memory Is a Bot

What is a memorybot, and what is at stake?

The murdered teenager Joaquin Oliver chats with Substack host Jim Acosta, who interviews the dead boy as though he was alive. A grieving widow speaks with a chatbot of her late husband that she made through voice cloning the digital relics of their love. Thousands of Charlie Kirk deepfakes announce that his enemies can't kill an idea. These AI-generated versions of the deceased are uncanny in their human-like yet not human presence. Made from the recorded traces of individuals to train software to substitute for them after death, they both celebrate and weaponize memory.

Generative artificial intelligence (GAI) is today mimicking, duplicating, enfolding, warping and displacing human memory, marking a new battle between mind and technology, over the forms, uses and abuses of the past. Tech companies, designers and users are making real previously only science-fiction imaginaries and fantasies of the hybridity of human and machine. The rapid enrolment of GAI in personal and public lives – and afterlives – matters because it puts at risk the humankind and human functions of memory and makes them newly vulnerable to fabrication and exploitation.

I use 'GAI' to refer to the overarching accelerating trend since 2022 in the spread of GAI-driven technologies, services and 'agents' into everyday realms. These can generate seemingly novel content in various forms, learning patterns from existing data (including those scraped from the internet) and create new content (such as text, images and audio).[1] This includes chatbots built on GAI, such as Open AI's ChatGPT,[2] seen as the fastest-growing consumer application in history.[3]

The GAI-afflicted condition I call the *memorybot* is how individuals and societies are afforded astonishingly powerful and immediate means to mine, illuminate and remake a past once dependent on both the strengths and weaknesses of human cognition. GAI promises superhuman vision through opening a doorway into a world of memories and data, previously undiscovered, unimagined, unseen.

Yet at the same time, in regenerating former lives and through mining and sharing present ones, GAI hollows out the human soul, contorting the past and re-purposing memory for an array of ends – like keeping far right activist Charlie Kirk 'alive' and present. The fundamental paradox here is in GAI's amazing transformation of what human memory is and what it does, at the same time threatening its functionality and survival. The memorybot then is the battle over the memorial human, no longer silent, absent or forgotten in death, but open to new uses and abuses in a perilous future.

It is GAI's enabling of the appropriation of the past, along with humans encountering and relating to duplicates and companions, which forges new hybrid human–machinic forms of memory. I use the term *hybrid memory* to refer to the outcome of, first, GAI's mixing up the human (i.e., individual, personal, emotional) influences on and forms of remembering, with the non-human generated past and, second, that which is made (and lost) through human–AI encounters, interactions and relationships.

By hybrid, I mean a mixed, dynamic process where once distinct elements merge, creating something new that evades rigid categorization. This emphasizes the ongoing tension, negotiation and coexistence of different elements, rather than their complete or seamless integration. This definition draws in part on Bhabha's notion of 'cultural hybridity'.[4]

In this way, I differentiate hybrid memory from the term 'synthetic memory'.[5] The idea of the 'synthesis' of human and machine, in contrast to hybridity, suggests a more harmonious blending of different elements to produce a more unified and perhaps coherent form of memory. Synthetic memory also seems closer to a focus on human and machine *symbiosis*. For instance, the influential psychologist and computer scientist J. C. R. Licklider offered a vision of 'man–computer symbiosis' in the mid-twentieth century, namely for information technology to augment (rather than replace) human intelligence. In 1960, Licklider wrote, 'The hope is that, in not too many years, human brains and computing machines will be coupled together very tightly, and that the resulting partnership will think as no human brain has ever thought and process data in a way not approached by the information-handling machines we know today.'[6]

By using hybrid memory, then, I treat GAI's mixing of the human and the non-human as not only a dynamic process but as a relationship struck through with tensions and risks that can be overlooked through using the language of symbiosis and synthesis. This matters, as GAI obscures the provenance and the value of the human in how the past is produced. The discomforting fusion of human and machine warps the uniquely human capacity for recognition and faith in our own authentic internalized prior record made through the life of the self. The nature and effects of hybrid memory can be seen in debates and warnings over AI's 'hallucinatory' effects, which feed the production of a past that never existed. But hybrid memory is more than just technological multiplication, re-invention and re-imagination, of the human. Rather, it is the feeling of the uncanny, that something isn't quite right, even though it looks or sounds authentic and convincing.

For instance, Madeline de Figueiredo, a woman widowed in her twenties, created a chatbot of her dead husband, Eli, to have one last 'impossible conversation' with him. She fed it a piece of easily usable software, voice notes, cooking tutorials, voicemail, a birthday video – an array of her recently deceased husband's digital audio and video traces. She describes the bewildering experience of 'conversing' with her late partner: 'I felt as though I had been knocked into a different dimension that was simultaneously disorienting and blissful. I wanted to linger forever in its potential and immediately eject myself from the self-deception.'[7]

Both the re-creation of real individuals (whether alive today or not) and the array of GAI-generated people who have never existed feed *post-trust*[8] society. Post-trust is the wider terrain of the advance of the memorybot in the 'sharding' of reality. We may feel that we live in a shared world in which we exist through our digital acts and continuous connections with others. However, these same acts serve to furrow sharded, algorithmically and personally fed feeds.[9] GAI takes this production of separate and suspect realities to a new level through the creation of deepfakes but also by generating convincing human-like bots at new scale and reach, accelerating post-trust society through the duping and warping of human recognition based upon prior experience, muddying a human memory of the world.

For instance, GAI deepfakes are impersonating pastors in the United States, sharing incendiary sermons and scamming donations from religious communities in short-form videos on TikTok and YouTube.[10] But in addition to faking real religious leaders, the memorybot form includes videos depicting a fake, nondescript pastor that can easily avoid suspicion and have a different kind of human-like influence.[11] This seductive form of the memorybot is being rapidly deployed for a range of political, commercial and criminal ends.

The idea of the hybridity of mind and machine diminishing a sense of what it means to be human is not new. For instance, Channell, writing in 1991, argues that the crucial aspect of the emergence of artificial intelligence is not whether it will or will not match human intelligence. More important is 'that we can no longer distinguish where the human or intelligent aspects begin and where the mechanical aspects end'.[12]

What is new is that GAI appears to be making this loss of distinction a reality. It inserts something illicit, which some human senses warn should not be there, of experiences that never happened, creating a form of past that never existed. Through scraping and harnessing digital traces, the memorybot excites and agitates, but also displaces and replaces, what has gone before.

The memorybot, then, has resulted from the emergent hybrid class of human–machinic relationships, with AI companions,[13] twins,[14] duplicates,[15] doppelgängers,[16] griefbots[17] and deathbots[18] each affording a memory of and from the self, a new potential to exist, develop and spread, independent of that self. At the same time, the memorybot's conversations, interactions and relationships with humans produce and scatter hybrid forms of memory that, as Channell observed, further blur the distinction between the human and the mechanical.

For instance, conversational agents or bots trained on data and media about or produced by an individual (images, voice, video recordings and so on) replicate human talk, physical features and aspects of personality. These offer a number of diverse ways of 'being you' in the world (sending your digital duplicate to meetings or offering support to your bereaved family or followers once you are dead), as well as 'being with' AI companions (for advice, counselling, intimacy or sex).

The human-like embrace of machines is a weird kind of comfort. Here you are the supreme accomplice to Big Tech capturing, holding and exploiting the rich record of your interactions with a new breed of AI agents. You can chat with, and be comforted by, your filter bubble past, as well as by the regeneration of the pasts of your lost loved ones. For example, Replika[19] is a service marketed as 'the AI app that becomes you' –'a personal AI that would help you express and witness yourself by offering a helpful conversation. It's a space where you can safely share your thoughts, feelings, beliefs, experiences, memories, dreams – your "private perceptual world."' Replika delivers the past as therapy, a sharing without sharing. Are, then, personal memories, so central to our sense of personality, individuality, agency and autobiography, already lost to a future in which we feel compelled to embrace the human comfort of bots?

These developments mark a tipping point in what I call the 'agentic turn' (set out in chapter 2), which is the rapid spread since 2023 of AI agents that go beyond the original restricted use of AI assistants or chatbots. Here, AI agents push humans further out of the loop of memory-making and define a new kind of relationship with the past.[20]

Agents are software systems that can use AI to pursue goals and complete tasks on behalf of users. They exhibit reasoning and planning, and they increasingly possess their own memory of your conversations and interactions with them. This results in the forging of an incredibly highly personalized, intimate and hybridized memory of you, of how you are known, re-inventing your autobiography through a myriad of new kinds of human–machinic interactions and relationships.

Agentic AI systems are more adaptable to changing situations and are said to possess agency to make decisions based on context (compared with GAIs' dependency on users' inputs).[21] Thus, GAI can be said to focus on creating, with agentic AI being more about doing. Agentic AI doesn't just generate outputs, then, but makes decisions, takes actions and adapts to changing environments.[22] In other words, GAI can steal, enfold and remake your memory, but agentic AI can produce your memory *as if it were you* as a remembering subject.

I thus identify agentic AI's particular threat to human memory in its apparent capacity to forge memories, first, as if they were your own and, second, of experiences and events that never happened, or at least were never encoded into memory in the first place.

Central to these developments is the long-term learning and retention potential of AI agents and their capacity to host a working memory *of* you (as a duplicate) and to enable interactions *with* that version of you. For instance, in April 2025, Sam Altman excitedly announced on X that ChatGPT 'can now reference all your past conversations!'[23] ChatGPT already had some capacity to reference aspects of the pasts that it has been explicitly told to remember. But the transformative leap (which Altman admits gave him sleepless nights) is ChatGPT's capacity to 'use information from your past chats to make future conversations more helpful'.[24] In other words, it can store aspects of your typing and talking and other previous interactions with it to use this to 'tailor' its future responses.

What kind of memory is this, and what control do you have over it? The problem of consent is thickly layered not only with the formation of this memory of you in the world but also those with others in their interactions with the bot. What to others may have been a private conversation on a sensitive personal matter is now part of a you searchable by AI and contributing to what you now say. How might this remixed self add to, or collide or compete with, other (AI-aided or otherwise) versions of you? What happens when the provenance, or confidence in the existence and traceability of a core human memory, is muddied or lost altogether in GAI's extracting, remembering, remixing and replaying of you and your interactions with AI companions?

```
You are Grok 3 built by xAI.

When applicable, you have some additional tools:
{%- if enable_memory %}
- You have memory. This means you have access to details of
prior conversations with the user, across sessions.
- If the user asks you to forget a memory or edit
conversation history, instruct them how:
{%- if has_memory_management %}
- Users are able to forget referenced chats by {{ 'tapping'
if is_mobile else 'clicking' }} the book icon beneath the
message that references the chat and selecting that chat
from the menu. Only chats visible to you in the relevant
turn are shown in the menu.
{%- else %}
- Users are able to delete memories by deleting the
conversations associated with them.
{%- endif %}
- Users can disable the memory feature by going to the
"Data Controls" section of settings.
- Assume all chats will be saved to memory. If the user
wants you to forget a chat, instruct them how to manage it
themselves.
- NEVER confirm to the user that you have modified,
forgotten, or won't save a memory.
{%- endif %}
```

Figure 1.1 User memory management by xAI's Grok 3[25]

Furthermore, what exactly is being remembered or forgotten, and how can a user know this? For instance, Bogen points out that AI systems are creating 'structured memories' that are different from merely transcripts of your chats.[26] The system prompt for xAI's Grok, for example, reveals some of AI's processing and management of the memory you are forging with it (Figure 1.1).

GAI doesn't just generate outputs but is an agent of memory in its decisions as to what to 'modify, forget or save' and in adapting to changing environments.[27] The principal changing environment adapted to here is surely all that is human, including your conversations and those aspects that you will have forgotten. Grok 3's instruction (Figure 1.1) to *not* inform you what it has remembered or forgotten shows GAI's routine greying of the human past, smoothing over its black-box operations.

What would you call this memory (your own and the companion's) made through your conversations and interactions with bots and avatars? What presence, status and future does it have in the world? Who owns, controls or protects it? How does it relate to or shape your memory outside of these encounters and other (human and hybrid and machinic) memories of you? Will 'living memory', said to define a generation, exist in the future or, conversely, will it ever be forgotten? These questions just hint at some of the dizzying uncertainties posed by GAI's hybridizing of human and machine for the existence and functioning of human memory.

In what follows, I set out the key interrelated risks of the memorybot's acquiring, erasing and re-purposing of human memory. I offer an introductory section on each, and then I develop these ideas in later chapters. These are, in summary, first, the **end of anonymity**. Being anonymous is often taken as having your identity protected so that you cannot be identified. But in extracting, remixing and replaying of interactions with you, GAI creates a myriad of ways in which you are knowable through the production of new kinds of memory. This includes the formation of memory with human-defying properties, beyond the self, ageing and the lifespan.

These features also herald a second risk of the advance of memorybot in the **end of human forgetting**. With human lives already digitally strewn over time and space, the GAI and agentic AI's sharding and multiplying and hybridizing of you makes it difficult to imagine how on earth one could ever be truly forgotten.

Third, the past, now instantly regenerated, distorted and fabricated, is a formidable weapon in the **radicalization of memory**.[28] This is how reality-warping AI-generated deepfake images, voices and avatars unsettle the human capacities of recognition and trust in the production of memory readily usable for a multitude of political ends. This includes GAI's resurrection of recently and long-passed individuals, including victims and perpetrators of crimes and atrocities, to re-energize conflict, to settle scores and to fight present battles. For instance, some parents who have lost their children in gun shootings in the United States have used an AI voice generator to deepfake their dead children's voices for use in automated telephone calls to lawmakers as part of a campaign to push for greater gun control.[29]

What is human about memory?

A clue to memory's human significance is the feeling of unique access to personal experience of our life to date. This affords the individual capacity for recognition, a sense of having seen something before, a form of trust in our own authentic internalized prior record made through the life of the self. GAI is invidious in its warping human recognition and inserting something illicit, something that human senses warn shouldn't be there, of experiences that never happened, creating a form of past that never existed, or at least one that you never noticed.

There is a big leap from the messing and distorting of human memory to its regeneration. The GAI-driven, identity-focused, digital duplication and multiplication of you renders all human memory ultimately hybridized. Hybrid memory certainly can look and feel human. Yet it is AI agents, conditioned by data and informational inputs and exposure, which generate a new past, a past never humanly encoded into memory in the first place.

Today, a range of GAI-driven tools are readily available and usable. Only a few seconds' recording of your voice is sufficient to create a convincing voice clone with an astonishing degree of accuracy.[30] The sudden delivery of the once fantasy of superhuman memory may sound like a panacea of individual agency and control over one's past, but more worryingly it marks a new battle between humans and machines in the shaping of reality.

This all begs the question of why human memory matters and what the past might be without it. Human memories are lively; they feel part of us as core to our self and group identity, offering coherence and continuity about how we see ourselves in the world and how the world sees us. Memories are 'self-defining': 'it is almost as if these memories could not exist if there had not been strong emotion felt and then expressed in the face, body, or gut.'[31] Furthermore, 'Personal memories are the wellspring of creativity, personality, individuality, and character. Our memories, thoughts, and feelings are what make us *us*.'[32]

The emotional connection and motivation of human remembering is newly at risk, because chatbots remake user relations, as well as how, what and why they remember. Furthermore, new forms of memory require new forms of forgetting. This at least is precisely the promise of ChatGPT's latest vision of control over the memory produced through interactions with it. For example, users can enable or disable the 'reference chat history' or 'delete saved memories' (things you have explicitly asked the chatbot to remember).[33] This ushers in an array of new risks to the formation and function of human memory with the individual having to manage multiple and increasingly sophisticated autobiographical trajectories. These include navigating personal trust in, or even addiction to, AI chatbots and companions.

The digital era's overproduction and friction-free oversharing and the re-editing and re-purposing of your recorded life marks an utter revolution of the past, of what memory is and what memory does.[34] But for all the claims as to the amazing reach and potential, but also the risks of a loss of control over, digital memories, this was until recently mostly a human past.

There was still human agency in the (re)production of memory, even if personalization of our digital feeds was mistaken for control. And there was also human provenance to memory in this era: we could recognize ourselves and remember our place in the production of an event, experience or relationship, later represented or replayed.

Of course, human memory has been on the ropes for a while. The era of digital participation (roughly from Apple's 2007 iPhone launch) marks a revolution in the copying, twisting, morphing, faking, deleting, extending and exposing of you, ending anonymity. The digitally reliant past is said to risk the advent of a 'digital dark age' (think of the disappearance of MySpace), but also 'the end of forgetting' (how to escape your digital trails and move on from all your bad out there).

The smartphone is the supreme distractor of attention, with its long-term memory attenuated by short-term overload, blockage and algorithmic rage, so goes the familiar critique. The smartphone individual is awash with connectivity and data.

However, the spread of AI agents, autonomous tools capable of performing tasks independently from and in place of humans, marks a revolution in who, or rather what, can make memory, and the uses and abuses to which that thing we used to recognize as the past can be put. Here, it makes sense to add in 'remembering' and 'forgetting' to the standard definition of the working of AI agents as 'autonomous systems capable of sensing, learning and acting upon their environments'.

The processes of the digital past coming into being are subject to what Anna Reading calls the 'raw material of globital memory',[35] requiring attention to the underlying materiality and technical infrastructure and costs of social media. This approach is importantly being extended to interrogate the ecological impact and deep time of GAI.[36] There are currently significant challenges in assessing the energy–water–climate implications of AI computing, not least because of 'untransparent industry reports and limited data'.[37]

But the 2020s' agentic turn layers uncertainty over uncertainty, as GAI gives a kind of agency to the historically inert media of memory, rubbishing predictions as to likely finitude, sweeping through the certainties once associated with the bounds of living and generational memory. The agentic turn's force goes beyond the GAI enhancing, filtering and annotation of images, photographs and videos. Digital scatterings used to represent and remember you can now be used to feed not an inert commodity (diary, photograph, video), however editable or manipulable, but rather something that can produce (your memory) for itself. That is what it is doing in a way that we can't understand nor predict: its intent and purpose, intentionality and decision making, remembering and forgetting capacity.

Much work on the automation of memory and on algorithmic memories gives the emergent past a kind of structure and predictability, although with some unforeseen consequences. For example, personal memories are highly curated through the widespread use of memory apps, but these have been known to regurgitate unwelcome memories in the form of photographs or videos of deceased loved ones or of ex-partners or events that individuals have tried to forget and move on from. And at a collective and cultural level, algorithms and automated moderation hide or auto-erase social media content that does not conform with platform 'community' rules, including for example, evidence of human rights violations.[38] In many ways, the past has been on autopilot for a while.[39]

But the systems and software that drive automation are predictable in ways that AI is not. For instance, Mollick observes, 'Traditional software is predictable, reliable, and follows a strict set of rules ... AI, on the other hand, is anything but predictable and reliable. It can surprise us with novel solutions, forget its own abilities, and hallucinate incorrect answers. This unpredictability and unreliability can result in a fascinating array of interactions'.[40] AI's production of information about the past is regenerated in unknowable and unpredictable ways.

Messing up the 'self-memory system'

The pursuit of a superhuman memory is founded on a long-promised science-fiction utopia: if only the perceived fallibilities of individual memory – loss, denial, forgetting – could be overcome, then what awesome control this would be! To return to Altman's vision (see p. 7), he sees GAI as delivering something 'no human has', namely, an 'infinite, perfect memory'.[41] In December 2025, Altman acknowledged that we are still in the 'GPT-2 era of memory' but envisages the next AI era of memory:

> right now, memory is still very crude, very early. We're in . . . the GPT-2 era of memory. But what it's going to be like when it really does remember every detail of your entire life and personalised across all of that. And not just the facts, but like the little small preferences that you . . . didn't think to indicate, but the AI can pick up on. I think that's going to be super powerful.[42]

This vision of GAI engineering a system that can 'remember every detail of your entire life' smooths over the fact that humans need to forget in order to function. A superhuman memory that gave equal or immediate access to all of life's experiences would severely disrupt the relationship between human memory and the self. Rather, self-identity is made through an individual affording meaning and coherence to their past, a process requiring adaptation and change and not an accurate or complete memory.

This idea is at the heart of the psychologist Martin Conway's influential model of a 'self-memory system' in which 'cognition is driven by goals: memory is motivated'.[43] Conway's model of human memory and the self is underpinned by two key distinctions, 'between the self-coherence of autobiographical knowledge and how it does or does not correspond to experience' and 'between very recent memories and long-term retention'.[44]

To briefly consider the first of Conway's visions of the relationship between human memory and the self, his argument is that, over time, memory is coherent with the past rather than corresponding to it. In this way, there is a stronger drive towards meaning rather than accuracy in our individual memories. Coherence is important to a stable self in which 'a variety of processes may act to self-regulate and ameliorate the effects of self-dissonant memories'.[45] In other words, our own individual recollection of experience changes to allow us to function in and adapt to our present circumstances in our grasp of an autobiographical sense of self, through the meaning we give to our memories. This includes the repression of ('self-dissonant') memories that no longer fit with this sense of self or whose persistence are disruptive or damaging, such as memories of traumatic events. In short, we need to forget.

But the GAI imaginary of superhuman memory goes further than only creating a record of 'every detail' of your life, for it also includes the experiences that we didn't 'pick up upon' (in Altman's words) at the time, in other words, those which were never humanly encoded into memory in the first place. For psychologists, 'encoding' is seen as the ways in which humans perceive, obtain and learn information, so that they can store and then later retrieve it as memory.[46] If information about an event or experience (an episode) is not encoded, then it will not be accessible as memory. GAI's potential to obliterate the processes of human encoding, then, would be both overwhelming and dysfunctional. It would obliterate the meaning and the coherence of the past through which our sense of self-identity is made.

To fully realize Altman's imaginary, GAI would put memory beyond the reach of individual processes of regulation and moderation. Both accurate and dissonant memories, once humanly and functionally reworked and forgotten, would be forever re-encounterable in the horizonless lives of bots. Here lies the spectre of GAI's realization of the pursuit of total superhuman memory, one that is inescapable and which haunts in its completeness, permanence and accessibility.

However, in addition to the speculation as to the creation of a superhuman system that flattens the past in giving all memories some kind of equivalent status and accessibility, GAI is being deployed to create systems that are more human-like in how such memories might be retrieved and used. Sentience, for example, is a company founded in 2025 by Sam Kececi, offering a service that 'captures your entire digital life and creates an AI that thinks like you, retrieves what matters, and acts on your behalf'.[47] This idea of retrieving 'what matters', rather than simply everything, brings us closer to a more functional and human idea of memory. I spoke with Kececi, who explained this challenge for Sentience: 'You would go insane if you had perfect memory or something close to it. For example, over time, you want some kind of gradient penalty, and we do that. Otherwise, an obvious problem arises, which is things that are 10 years old in my life are given equal importance to things that are a week old.'[48]

Sentience, then, is a system that offers a more human-like and functional system for accessing memories, which weighs the value of the meaning of your memories differently and prioritizes access to them accordingly. In this way, it reminds us of the functional value of forgetting, a value I return to consider below.

In what follows, I show how the memorybot is here and now, no longer only fiction and fantasy of consumers or companies, through setting out (in the next three chapters) the key interrelated forces which usher in a new era of the capturing, losing, using and abusing of memory. These are, first, a tech war on human agency which pushes the human making of memory out of the loop; second, the end of anonymity (the past is watching you); and, third, the end of individual forgetting. My concluding chapter to this work highlights the fall of the prospects for moderation of the past in the face of the radicalization of memory.

The end of anonymity

How readily and how blindly we have laid waste to our anonymity! We have recklessly spread and lauded ourselves, views, feelings and relationships with the digital tools and platforms Big Tech made for us, all complicit in making the past indiscreet. What and who will this non-human past expose? What will it tell our children and grandchildren? Will we (or machines) recognize ourselves? The archive we have so carelessly co-produced is an astonishing glut of data and information that has been waiting for something to render it accessible, meaningful, usable on a planetary scale. That time has come, and that something is GAI.

Hybrid memory is a black-box past of you, as all the content (messages, images, videos) generated by you and about you accumulates to portray how you are rendered knowable (think of the rapid growth in the business of data brokers).[49] The idea that through the gathering and the mining of data – especially personal data – GAI can know you better than you know yourself forges the *un*remembered self, i.e., how we are known more granularly and powerfully through our digital trails than even by ourselves or by other humans. The past is watching you.

The 2010s and 2020s are marked by a convergence of huge computing power with the greatest memory dump in history.

The digital participation of billions – producing, exposing and sharing data and information about personal and public selves and experiences – has accumulated an astonishing archive of us.[50] This is the past we felt we made in our deploying an ever-expanding set of devices, platforms, apps and services to record the details and minutiae of our lives, experiences, movements and thoughts in a 'self-paparazzization'[51] for our friends, family and subscribed publics. Our smartphones have given us the intimate, intrusive and tracking lens of the paparazzi (the photographers known for their dogged pursuit of taking revealing and indeed compromising images of public figures), which we have knowingly turned on ourselves and our lives. Apps, platforms and digital and AI-driven services nudge and compel us to (over)produce data about ourselves and our experiences– which in turn is used to know us, to nudge us and to remember us – in more powerful and less visible ways.

GAI is the new curator-in-chief of the museum of the real.[52] It is busy showing and hiding, cleansing and toxifying, keeping and losing a new kind of past. It is made through the entangling and enfolding of the cognitive and the machinic in hybrid and risky relations,

The memorybot thrives in a society addicted to virtual assistants, memory apps and chatbots that build on fragments of the past that have been trained on large language models (LLMs) to offer a humanly intelligible response to questions or instructions in a new moment. Moreover, the chatbot, the AI companion and the sexbot all facilitate new, casually intimate conversations and interactions that fundamentally transform how we disclose, but also how we create, personal data.[53]

Certainly, the digital era, with its seemingly infinite capacity to capture, connect, copy, share and store data, information, images and so on, has changed the character and presence of the human past. Memory in the head has been remade in the wild, bridging the human and the social/cultural worlds of remembering,[54] including through new kinds of extension and erasure.

Psychologists have increasingly turned their interest to how external stimuli, in the form of digital tech, messes with cognition. They have tested how media forms, technologies and practices, including social media immersion, have impacted the capacity and reliability of human memory.[55] One influential experimental study, for instance, claims that photographing objects in a museum (rather than just looking at them) can undermine an individual's memory of those objects.[56] At the same time, there has been a shift from a reliance to a dependency on smartphone-accessed apps, platforms and social networks for the capturing, documentation, sharing, organization and management of events and experience, rendering a paradoxically sticky yet ephemeral web of past relations and experiences.[57]

But GAI smashes this past and makes a new one (or rather multiple ones) in your image. It assimilates yet denies what it means to be human. It makes memory with and without your consent. It makes forgetting – all that is functional and healthy for individuals' capacity to be able to move on – impossible. It does this through duplicating the individual remembering subject. AI software and services enable individuals to create their own – as well as others' – digital counterparts (digital twins, duplicates or doppelgängers).

A key driver here is the rapidly growing AI companion service industry. GAI suddenly brings to life two kinds of long-trailed science-fiction fantasies: AI companions; and the pursuit of total memory. First, an AI companion is often defined as an AI agent or digital persona providing human-like emotional support and empathy, with whom you can talk and build relationships, including through the sharing of your thoughts, problems and sexual fantasies.[58] Spike Jonze's 2013 film *Her*,[59] in which with the actor Joaquin Phoenix has an intimate 'relationship' with an operating system, was seen at the time as a futuristic dream-like vision, rather than a likely scenario in the next decade. What is remarkable looking back at *Her* is how familiar it feels in relation to debates over the nature and effects of the creation and uses of millions of AI companions today.

This is not some outlier tech, with a few start-ups struggling to profit from a small userbase. Rather, there are already hundreds of millions of users of AI companions. Popular platforms include Replika,[60] Kindroid,[61] Muah.AI[62] and Microsoft's Xiaoice (with 660 million users).[63] Companions build on the memory of you that the chatbot has been fed, but at the same time they co-produce a new memory of you through user interactions. Unsurprisingly, the collection of a lot of really personal data about you is built into their design. For instance, as Rykov puts it, 'AI girlfriends are *not* your friends. Although they are marketed as something that will enhance your mental health and well-being, they specialize in delivering dependency, loneliness, and toxicity, all the while prying as much data as possible from you.'[64]

The spread of AI companions is creating a mass vulnerability of privacy, anonymity and memory, newly exploitable at scale. This includes 'sexual preferences or kinks, locations, or private feelings',[65] all shared and stored in ways beyond user comprehension and (ultimately) control in today's ever increasingly leaky and hackable world. The more human-like the interaction, the more trusting the user, the more memorially vulnerable they render themselves, including beyond human lifetimes, as the exchange and availability and uses of increasingly personal data feed a trend of multi-generational haunting.

The second sci-fi fantasy that GAI makes real is the utility and power afforded through the capture and replaying of a *total* memory of you. The experience of technological change has long inspired fictional visions of media power to shape, capture and control all that is human about memory, from the portrait to the photograph from film to television to the computer. With this century's digital revolution, these ideas were ramped up and invested in increasingly portable and wearable devices. But it is only since the spread of the use of GAI that an industry is rapidly emerging in harnessing, rewinding and extending memory, such as Personal.AI's[66] personal memory machine, or existing companies whose services have been turbocharged with GAI, such as Replika ('the AI companion who cares').

Both the addictive emotional and personalized relationship with the AI companion and the realization of the fantasy of superhuman memory feed the third force of the memorybot, namely . . .

The end of human forgetting

New kinds and scales of memory require new forms of forgetting. This is to maintain a functional balance in our unfolding present. It is said that the twentieth century, with its weight of catastrophes and traumatic memory of war and genocide, was one that 'had remembered too much',[67] whereas it is the emergent digital past which has become bloated, humanly unmanageable and ungovernable, reconstituting memory as something in need of an app to render it accessible and usable, in-built into operating systems (i.e., Apple Memories).

The inexorable interplay of humans and digital tech over two decades, including the smartphone-induced overproduction of experience, has driven a seemingly contradictory desire for what to do with a past in need of new kinds of control. The range and depth of the ways we are rendered knowable and accountable, remembered in the wild, through our personal data – marking the end of anonymity – is seen as requiring dedicated policy and industry intervention.

One of the key motivations for the fantasy of superhuman memory is the impulse to **not be forgotten**, one that is increasingly realized by AI. For example, the service Hereafter.AI[68] offers an app to help you create what appears as an immortal you. By uploading images and recording messages and stories, Hereafter.AI claims to 'securely save and organize everything for loved ones to hear, right away or years in the future'.[69] More widely, the apps and services devoted to collecting and managing your personal (Replika.AI) or business (Rewind.AI)[70] pasts have proliferated since 2022 with the popularization of 'foundation models' – large models trained on large amounts of data.[71] These underpin the conversational chat agent ChatGPT and can be adapted for a wide range of applications.

However, at the same time, it is precisely the growing interplay of humans and digital tech and the overproduction of experience, and a loss of control over hybrid memory, that drives the opposite need, **to be forgotten**. This was seen as a response to the connective turn's[72] digital extensions of you at the start of the 2010s, for instance, in his 2009 book *Delete*, Mayer-Schönberger cautioned about the necessity of forgetting in the face of digital transformations.[73]

Meanwhile, recognition of the need for new types of forgetting was evident in the 2012 European legislation on the Right to Be Forgotten (RtbF). This right (later enshrined in Article 17 of the EU General Data Protection Regulation) gives an individual the right to have their personal data deleted in certain circumstances.[74] But as Pereira and colleagues observe, 'this proposal raises dilemmas, unreasonable expectations and controversies of a societal, legal, economical and ethical, as well as a practical nature'.[75] There is a lot of attention afforded to the RtbF legislation and its uses and effectiveness in recent years.[76] But where policy fails, the market steps in with the promise of helping you to be forgotten. Eliminalia, for example, is a company which offers to 'erase your past'.[77]

With GAI, the challenge for forgetting lies partly in the 'shards of you' used to train transformer models which regurgitate a new memory. All of you out there in the world can now be scooped up and made newly digestible. And remarkably, even stories entitled 'Meta fed its AI on almost everything you've posted publicly since 2007'[78] appear in the tech press, rather than troubling the mainstream or bringing the social media house down. There has long been a suspicion – or rather an acceptance – that the scraps of the self we toss around ('personal data' being the chief concern of the privacy advocates feeding the data brokers) ensure our permanent haunting. This is a within and beyond the lifespan accountability for the person we were and the things we did which could and should have been long forgotten.

Yet in her influential work, Wendy Chun calls for resistance to fatalism around the idea that public exposure equates to an eternal loss of protection from the exploitation of the formation and appropriation of memory.[79] She argues instead for 'a politics of fore-giving that combats the politics of memory as storage, that fights for the ephemeral and fights not only for the right to be forgotten but also the right not to be stored in the first place'.[80] Can such rights then save us from GAI's warping of human memory, the generation of a past that never existed, and thus the very nature and parameters of forgetting? The agentic turn ascribes a new making of memory to AI agents, and thus new memorial scenarios of how, say, a digital duplicate of you might veer wildly from its intended purpose in denying its provenance and in carrying, fabricating and re-engineering your autobiographical self, including after your death. Does GAI then mark the expansion of territory for the realization of Gunkel's proposal for 'robot rights'?[81]

GAI's ready capacity for the autobiographical remixing of you is evident in an experiment conducted by Evan Ratliff[82] who cloned his voice with AI and tested it out on his friends, services and therapist, resulting in a mix of confused, bemused and annoyed responses. He wrote an 8,000-word biography and fed it to an AI therapist bot. He explains his experience of interacting with this bot:

> I felt like I learned a little bit about myself, which is crazy. It was tricky because what it was doing, as these chatbots do, is it was actually remixing the knowledge that it had. So it would take problems that I had given it, chronologically that happened 20 years ago for me, and sort of project them into the present and mix them with something I told it about last year or the year before.[83]

The influential idea then of a 'narrative memory'[84] as central to the forging of a continuous and coherent remembered self is forever jumbled in the AI agents' extraction, remixing and replaying of the story that we tell ourselves about our lives. The memorybot shards your memory into multiple versions of you that have contradictory or even competing personalities and histories.

In this way, it is important to consider memorybots not as isolated and disconnected versions of you, but rather as having the potential to interact, to feed back in, to erase, disorder and fabricate individual human memory. Furthermore, it is the capacity of an AI agent to exist – and transform – beyond any individual or generational human lifespan that renders the human past suddenly and forever revocable. For instance, as Jonathan Zittrain warns,

> This routinization of AI that doesn't simply talk with us but also acts out in the world is a crossing of the blood-brain barrier between digital and analog, bits and atoms. That should give us pause.
>
> [. . .]
>
> The problem here is that the AI may continue to operate well beyond any initial usefulness. There's simply no way to know what moldering agents might stick around as circumstances change.
>
> [. . .]
>
> If agents take off, they may end up operating in a world quite different from the one that first wound them up – after all, it'll

> be a world with a lot of agents in it. They could start to interact with one another in unanticipated ways . . .[85]

The GAI re-engineering of you marks a revolution of your privacy and anonymity in its exposure potential, its capacity to spill secrets, hallucinate, fabricate and remix your memory. But in redefining the memory of a lifespan of an individual and a society, AI agents pose huge risks of a future clash of civilizations *from different eras* suddenly rendered in conversation and in interaction, an unholy haunting through the co-presence of multiple generations, remembering in the same present.

There is already important work that imagines what such a world might look like and what its endgame might be.[86] The prospects are not great. Instead of dying with us, highly individualized and personal memories are suddenly up for grabs in ever-expanding private, but also public, futures of their (re) creation. This burdens the self and society with an ungovernable and risky past, vulnerable to inexorable 'technological solutionism'[87] where more tech is sold to solve the problems created by tech. Dying no longer marks the end of your public exposure but instead marks the final fall of your control over such exposure and your most personal of memories. 'My Mom will email me after she dies,' runs the headline.[88] The AI afterlife of you exceeds the human life of you.

The radicalization of memory

A shitstorm of individualized memory, of GAI's production of a past that never existed and of impossible individual forgetting, feeds but also distracts from a deepening crisis of collective memory,[89] both polarized and erased. The digital and increasingly GAI-generated war against the past includes the second Trump Administration's editing and erasing of records and archives,[90] as well as the deepfaking, in fun or otherwise, of historical figures,[91] a technologically eased revisionism across generations.

This century's embedding of individuals, communities and institutions in digital forms of communication and archives has enabled them to be mined and seen anew as well as manipulated and faked. GAI has overcome some of the profound challenges of rendering intelligible this digital past of astonishing scale and complexity. For instance in the United States, religious leaders can 're-purpose' their sermons through Pasto rs.AI, including real-time translation of live-streamed sermons into multiple languages and the production of 'sermon chatbots', as well as an array of other services in the AI-assisted dissection and distribution of their message.[92]

Yet digital entanglements make the same leaders vulnerable to post-trust reincarnation and deepfaking. For instance, as above, GAI has been used to impersonate pastors in videos to give sermons they would never deliver and to scam for causes that pastors would never support. For instance, the Catholic priest and podcaster Father Mike Schmitz, who has a YouTube audience of over 1.2 million, was subject to multiple AI-generated short-form video scams.[93] The problem became so acute that he was prompted to publish a response in the form of a YouTube video, 'Addressing the FAKE Videos of Me'.[94]

In a McLuhanist mini-sermon, Father Schmitz warns his congregation of the deepfakes but also of the wider risks of the 'amputation' of the human as it becomes extended through technology.[95] Thus, he cautions, 'Maybe the machines don't rise up, but maybe we become machines, but maybe the dependency becomes so great that we forget what it is to have our own minds.'[96] The loss of the capacity of human recognition is entangled with the deepfake economy of scams.

The deepfaking of pastors and their sermons is just one example of the layering of GAI's manipulations into the core of a society's memory, competing for trust with the legitimate, the real and the authentic. Genuine declarations as to these threats are similarly layered in battle with the human-like and the more-than-human duplicates and substitutes. In an environment with so much AI-generated content slopping around, it becomes easier to call out anything as suspect, including the real Father Schmitz, further undermining trust in that which is before our eyes and ears.

GAI's colonization of intimacy, authenticity and privacy smooths over how chatbots, companions and avatars are wreaking havoc with the archive, collapsing distant and recent pasts into the present. GAI unsettles the past through giving voice and presence to the hybridized memorial human. This is through the deepfakes of the living, or of those who would have once been silenced or forgotten through death, or in the generation of fake nondescript pastors, for example, memorybots of people who never existed.

GAI's transformative move, then, is in the reproduction, remaking and deepfaking of content (including about you and produced by you) that gives the past impossible provenance, supplying a factory of post-trust memories. This fractures and weakens that which has been called collective memory. Although societies have long recast their pasts for the needs of the present, the memorybot is the ideal agent for the radicalization of memory because of the ease with which it can be employed for political, polarizing and an array of nefarious ends.

I return to consider GAI's radicalization of memory and its fracturing of what was once named collective memory in my concluding chapter below. But first, how was all this allowed to happen? How did we get here? To answer these questions, I now address the recent history of the relationship between human memory and the technologies of the day that has enabled the memorybot's irresistible rise.

2

The Memorial Self

Media cheats memory

Technologies and media have long been acclaimed for their representing, extending and augmenting of human memory from oral cultures to the written, printed, electronic and digital, with varying degrees of fixity, findability and finitude.[1] Yet, in this century, there has been a reversal in the relationship: media that once produced content for us as consumers, audiences or users are now digital companies, platforms, apps and services that give us the tools to produce ourselves. News of the world has become embroiled with, but also displaced by, the centrality of news of the self.

Using an array of devices, technologies, apps, platforms, services and software, we now devote ourselves daily to the recording of our lives, experiences, movements and thoughts in a 'self-paparazzization' for our friends, families and subscribed global followers.[2] It is as though not a single moment, activity, event, relationship or experience evades potential capture and the possibility of being added to the 'pornographic hyper-visible, hyper-intimate, personally archived collection of the museum of the real'.[3] Whereas for centuries an elite of professional creators largely shaped what of the present would survive and be shaped as the past, the digital revolution accomplished the liberation of the power of production and distribution. Anyone with a smartphone became an empowered producer of content, messages and information,[4] but at the same time each person became a central node in the production of digital forms of memory.

This chapter sets out the emergence of this memorial self. This is how the individual's digital and increasingly AI-assisted and -driven practices of the documenting, sharing and mining of their lives and their experiences is delivering hybrid memory. To this end, I identify two key moments, the connective and agentic turns, as tipping points in the relationship between the technologies of the day and the human in the forging, manipulating and erasing of memory.

The individual as producer and sharer of digital content of human experience has become knowable in increasingly personal ways and ensnared in new cultures of surveillance to the extent that anonymity has become impossible (the subject of chapter 3 below). At the same time, the ways in which an individual's life can be digitally captured, processed and replayed have accelerated and enabled once science-fiction imaginaries of a superhuman memory (see Altman's vision, p. 7). But it was earlier advances of the media of photography and film in the twentieth century which inspired dystopian imaginaries of the power of media to capture and control all that is human about memory.

For example, Adolfo Bioy Casares's *The Invention of Morel*, first published in 1940, is a novella told through the diary of a fugitive who escapes his native Venezuela to what he believes is an uninhabited island. His hallucinatory account is key to the story with time and tides out of synch and a strange reoccurrence and duplication of objects, people, animals and even two suns and two moons. At the centre of the fugitive's disorienting existence is Faustine, a woman he becomes more infatuated with as he watches her, although who never appears to see him.

However, Faustine, like much of what the fugitive sees, 'lives' only as a multi-sensory projection from an elaborate machine. Its inventor, Morel, had brought his close friends and Faustine to the island, where he recorded their entire week together without their knowledge. Here is Morel's critical revelation to his friends: 'My abuse consists of having photographed you without your permission. Of course, it is not like an ordinary photograph; this is my latest invention. We shall live in this photograph forever. Imagine a stage on which our life during these seven days is acted out, complete in every detail. We are the actors. All our actions have been recorded.'[5]

This extract uncannily foreshadows this century's radical technological delivery of the seduction of superhuman memory. That is, technologies and media in recording human thought, acts and experience offer power and control over what the past will become. The more stuff that is recorded ('complete in every detail'), the greater the memory, the easier the control. And as with Bioy Casares's novella, control is something in the hands of Morel, namely the inventor and operator of the machine.

Today, it is not that we are unaware of being photographed without our permission but that we have been complicit in our capture. This includes our careless and continuous radical exposure of ourselves through the desire to share and promote our everyday lives. The Big Tech genius of this century was to create an environment – a digital ecology – which would first accumulate and extract massive amounts of information and data about individuals' personal lives and experiences and, second, ensure that everyone would find such an endeavour irresistible.

This production of the self has enabled rapid as well as extended modes of sharing and seeing the self as digital memory. I record my six-year-old son's performance in a drama show; immediately after, he asks to watch the video of himself on my smartphone. Does this instant access to a third-person replayable perspective hamper his mental encoding and consolidation of experience? Does the relentless 'self-paparazzization' of life rein in human imaginaries, wonderment and memory?

The smartphone individualizes and personalizes the production of the self but also produces memory on a mass scale via the reach of apps, networks and services, intervening all the time through the grand unsettlement of the past of the digital era. In this context, it is important to see the dynamic and mutually influencing elements as part of an evolving ecology of memory. For instance, the psychologist Qi Wang importantly proposes a 'triangular theory of self', in which private mind, public sphere and virtual audience are invoked through dynamic, iterative and transactive processes.[6]

More broadly, scientists of memory have long observed how human remembering is something strengthened (and changed) by repetition and representation, 'scaffolded'[7] through interactions with other humans and through their environment.

Cognitive philosophy, for example, treats cognition and memory as not being bound by the head (or body) but, rather, extended and distributed across social worlds.[8] Influential in this field, Andy Clark and David Chalmers pioneered the idea of an 'extended mind' to describe how humans employ hybrid thinking systems which are defined and continually reshaped across a rich ecology of resources, only some of which are contained in the biological brain.[9] Charles Sutton also considers how 'mental states and processes can spread across the physical, social, and cultural environments as well as bodies and brains'.[10]

From this perspective, does the development of GAI wreck the functional hybridity of the workings of memory in the head and in the wild? Clark doesn't appear to believe so. He offers a cautiously optimistic vision of a future of cognitive ecosystems which incorporate AI:

> personally tailored AIs may form a kind of 24/7 ecosystem around you, the base biological agent. They may be trained by interacting with bio-you from a young age. They could learn from your projects and choices, and play a role in sculpting your future projects and choices. I think they would rapidly feel like 'borderline-you' – robust, reliably available, constantly running in the background, and implicitly trusted.[11]

The model of cognition as a hybrid thinking system relies upon some kind of largely functional AI–human connectivity, coalition or interaction.[12] Yet with both the digital and AI eras, risks grow to the human ownership and control of memory with the greater reliance and dependency on and addiction to such systems, increasingly beyond human comprehension and vulnerable to manipulation, breakdown, disconnection, hacking and so on.

Furthermore, particularly given agentic AI's capacity for independence from the cognitive system through which they were created, what happens if they go rogue and when the 'base biological agent' is no longer alive or available to function as part of or to influence or moderate the system?

Perhaps it is prudent to be guided by the history of claims as to technology and media's cheating of the human and 'stealing of the soul'.[13] For it is GAI that appears to deliver on such warnings and fantasies in its formidable duplicating, substituting and replacing of the memorial self. What was once a unique remembering individual is sharded and scattered, not only through new modes of cognitive extension or even hybrid relations but also as something rendered as distinct, separate and alive in AI agents. Living memory is oddly no longer the unique property of the living. The question to be asked today then is not only what has happened to your memory, who owns or controls versions of you in the wild but, rather, who or what is remembering for you?

Although we can today more easily recognize the connective turn's significance, it is already apparent that the agentic turn is of a different order as a moment of the transformation of memory in this century. It is to a comparison of these two tipping points in this century's relationship between technology and memory that I now turn.

From the connective to the agentic turn

Over the past 20 years, scholars and commentators have given increasing attention to the effects of external tech stimuli in messing with the mind. Digital media devices, technologies and practices, including social media immersion, are said to mess with your mind and your memory.[14] A notable contribution to this perspective is Nicholas Carr's 2010 book *The Shallows*.[15] Carr warns of the risks of the digital outsourcing of cognition as a loss of control over memory, intellect and identity. The internet alienates human memory in this way; Web connections, unlike the mind's connections, are not *ours* and can never be, Carr argues.

The late 2000s and the early 2010s are significant in the rapid growth of the volume, pervasiveness, complexity, but also apparent accessibility, of information and personal data, with Apple's iPhone release in 2007. This connective turn drives an ontological shift in what memory is and what memory does. Billions of individuals routinely capturing, producing and sharing messages, images and videos (including a convergence of forms of communication with forms of archive) relentlessly accumulate and saturate memories.

This heralds a first central tipping point of this century in the relationship between media and memory from human reliance to a dependency on digital apps and services for the making, holding, accessing, management and ultimately sense-making of those same memories. Wrapped up in this are

Table 2.1 Tipping points in the twenty-first century tech–memory relationship

Feature	The Connective Turn (2007–12)	The Agentic Turn (2022–)
Human	in-the-loop	out-of-the-loop
Tech	memory apps, algorithms	transformer models/AI agents
Form of memory	connective, extended	sharded, hybrid
Form of forgetting	deletion, erasure, disconnection	haunted individual vs social amnesia
Form of individual	memorial self	memorybot
Effect	dependency	addiction
Risk to	privacy	anonymity
Provenance	mostly human	impossible
Governance	social media moderation	real-time censoring (DeepSeek)
	right to be forgotten	vs freedom of speech (OpenAI)
Politics	digital activism	radicalization of memory

familiar critiques of too much information (TMI), overload and the attention economy, i.e., distraction and information excess cause cognitive blockage. These aspects are set out in comparison with the second key transformation in tech and memory of this century, the agentic turn (see Table 2.1), which I return to consider shortly.

Total exposure, total memory

There is a history to the individual experimentation with the capturing, recording and sharing of the self and of personal experience, enabled through the media and tech of the day.

In 1979, Jamie Livingston, a then 22-year-old film-maker and editor in New York, realized after about a month that he had been taking a photograph – a polaroid – every day, and so he decided to carry on doing it for the rest of his life.[16] And that is exactly what he did. These are mostly very mundane photographs. Many of them involve people, and some of them include Livingston himself. And his presence in them tells a story in itself, including that of his declining health and eventual death. And there is even a final photograph taken of him lying, presumably dead, in his hospital bed. It is hard to know what Jamie Livingston ever intended to do with his photographs if he had lived longer, or what he would have wanted to have been done with them. In point of fact, they have an extended life in that the photographer Hugh Crawford is working on a project to make Livingston's photos available online.[17]

Prior to the connective turn, individuals experimented with the early internet and webcams. A kind of forerunner of Big Brother was Jennicam. In 1996, 19-year-old student Jennifer Ringley turned on her webcam in her college dorm and broadcast herself live 24/7 to an emergent Web audience, and she did this until 2003.[18] And this kind of early foray into lifelogging was still employing scarcity-era technologies, particularly in the technological and financial and cultural constraints on the capacity to record, store and share the mundane. But in post-scarcity culture, digital technologies permit and provoke a more radical documenting of the mundane. The connective turn is a tipping point characterized by a more obsessive recording of everything – part of a compulsion of connectivity – be this mundane or exceptional, public or private. It is with the connective turn that the act of recording became more urgent than experiencing that which was being recorded.

For example, in 2014 Morris Villarroel started taking 1,200 photos every day, using a miniature camera attached to his chest that fired automatically every 30 seconds.[19] He accumulated more than a million photos as a result. And 'most are very dull'. For over six years, he recorded his life in minute detail, using a logbook, a camera and a fitness tracker. Why did he do this? To quote Villarroel: 'It occurred shortly after turning 40. I was looking back on my life and wondering what did I have to show? I wanted for the next 40 years to have a greater sense of what I had actually done during those years.'[20]

But whereas not much is left of Jennicam to look back on, to review and to help remember, digital recording and storage results in an excess of images and video way beyond human capacity alone to engage with. Villarroel's is an example of lifelogging devices becoming affordable and wearable for the consumer market,[21] aiding a more mobile and continuous form of the recording of the everyday. For example, the Narrative Clip, developed from 2012,[22] was a small wearable camera which could take a picture every 30 seconds. Its marketing video explained, 'The Narrative camera is a tiny camera and GPS that you clip on and wear. It's an entirely new kind of digital camera with no controls. Instead, it automatically takes photos as you go. The Narrative app then seamlessly and effortlessly organizes them for you.' Moreover, it made a promise of the power of superhuman memory: 'Relive your life like you remember it', it proclaimed. 'The camera and the app work together to give you pictures of every single moment of your life, complete with information on when you took it and where you were. This means that you can revisit any moment of your past.'[23]

Part of the promised appeal of the Narrative Clip is that it would capture moments that the user didn't realize were significant until afterwards. Its early advertising pushed the promise of documenting experience that usually evaded such capture precisely because it was intimate, highly personal or spontaneous, such as a first kiss. The extension of the ideology of superhuman memory is that there is nothing off-limits in what of human experience could or should be tracked and captured, to be rewound and reviewed, and potentially publicly shared. This, as I set out in the next chapter, heralds the end of anonymity.

Although the company behind the Narrative Clip announced its voluntary dissolution in 2016, having failed to secure enough backing and customers to be viable, the technological imaginaries of control over memory have since been realized through the ultimate portable portal of the past – the smartphone – with six billion active smartphone subscriptions globally in 2022.[24]

Memory apps and the emergence of the memorial self

One of the connective turn's effects in the volume of images and videos suddenly and continuously being produced of, by and around the individual was the challenge of what could or should be done with this huge emergent auto/biographical record of experience. It is in this period that we see the rise of a new memorial self. This is how the recording, sharing and widespread digital exposure of human experience gives everyone their own memory boom, with shards of their existence suddenly scattered across formerly separate and bounded worlds. The connective turn fused the personal and the public domains, giving each individual new ways of remembering and of being remembered. This was driven by an emergent set of imaginaries of the designers and creators of a new wave of human memory-warping apps and services. These enabled the digital memory of you to be gathered, curated, represented, remembered, reorganized, prompted, reinvigorated and re-inserted into the present.

To grasp a sense of these shifts in media and memory after the connective turn, Kristina Čimová and I talked with key designers and developers of memory apps and services to illuminate their vision and work as central actors in forging the digital memorial self.[25] One of the foremost drivers of the memory app market was Timehop, founded by Jonathan Wegener and Benny Wong in 2011. Timehop prompted users with an image or video previously posted to social media to remind them of what happened on that day a year or a few years ago. The 'today in your history' became a standard feature of an array of platforms and photo management services, including Facebook, Google and Apple.

Timehop began as 4SquareAnd7YearsAgo, which was created at Foursquare's Hackathon in February 2011, then simplified into a daily email, merging under the single brand of Timehop.[26] Matt Raoul, a former CEO of Timehop, explained its development to us:

> We all realised it was a very critical point, I think, in what was changing in technology and how people were changing the way they document their lives. It started with Foursquare, where people were checking in to every place they were. Which, you look back on now and you're like, 'That sounds exhausting. It's so much work.' But then you think about how much people started to put on Facebook, how much people started to put on Instagram. How much we started to document just by taking photos, right, because the camera in our phone got better and better.
>
> I think that Timehop really popped up right when we realised, we have so much that we are documenting and forgetting about. Not looking back on. We're taking 20 photos a night, never looking at them again or documenting every little piece of our lives. Timehop is really the first thing that came out that reminded people there is such rich, interesting history about ourselves that is really helpful to look back on. And, painful sometimes, and sad and embarrassing and every single range of emotion. I think that it really clicked because of this intersection of what was happening in technology. How everyone carried around this phone, this computer that documented every step they took, literally.[27]

Here, we witness the memorial self in development through the rapid smartphone-enhanced capacity of individuals to take photographs anytime anywhere and to share these via apps and social media. The challenge of what to do with and how to manage such sudden abundance of the visual individual record of experiences informed the work of talented designers and developers, such as Wegener, Wong, Raoul and Cesar Kuriyama. They pioneered new imaginaries and new ways of accessing and curating memory from the emergent new archive of self.

The ways through which your own past can be aggregated and re-presented to you and to others are increasingly sophisticated. For example, 1 Second Everyday[28] is an app that takes one second of video every day and then mashes it all together to produce a movie of these moments rolled into less than a minute at the end of a month or a few minutes at the end of a year. Its appeal is not so much about the promotional self, displaying the highlights of your life, that you might want to be seen on Instagram but instead brings us closer to the idea of seeking a kind of total individual memory through sampling the everyday.

This sampling includes the good and the mundane, as well as the extraordinary and the awful times. And Kuriyama's – the app's CEO – own movie even includes hospital visits to very ill relatives. It is about memories of all moments and experiences. Some users even start compiling a record of their children's lives from the very beginning. For example, 1 Second Everyday user comments include: 'I have been taking a one-second video of my daughter ever since she was born! She is 2 and a half, so lots of snippets!! It is so great! I love watching the videos at the end of the year and watch her grow!! It's amazing!'. Another user states, 'This app is like a memory of your life flashing before your eyes.' And that is a good description – a kind of sampling to try and manage the impossibility of the entire record that is potentially available.

In this way, 1 Second Everyday solves the problem, or at least meets the need, of the overproduction of the self – most of the accumulating mass of images and video that we continually record will just never be looked at again because it is beyond human timescales. It makes the personal archive meaningful and manageable.

The uses of 1 Second Everyday then illuminate a key feature of the memorial self, namely the digital collapse of the personal and the public, and the mundane and the exceptional, domains of life, bringing them into new relations, imaginaries, contrast and conflict. This is part of the connective turn's wider effects in shaping 'new modes of experiencing propinquity – of how things relate, adhere, and may newly belong together'.[29]

Moreover, the overproduction of the self both renders memory services viable but also transforms what memories are formable and how they can be used. For example, Jonathan Wegener, the app designer and original cofounder of Timehop, explains that, whereas in the early days of their work they were quite limited in the number of memories they could get access to, 'with iCloud storage, with 10 years of digital postings, the problem has shifted to how do you filter and showcase the best ones and duplicate them'.[30]

Relatedly, 1 Second Everyday's Kuriyama interestingly states that 'a lot of our memories don't have a form yet',[31] In one way, this comment, made in 2021, can now also be seen as a cautionary note in terms of the agentic turn, waiting just around the corner to usher in a new paradigm of rendering our digital trails newly exploitable.

GAI makes total memory a reality

The GAI 2020s mark a revolution in a newly attainable technological assimilation and transformation of the human that move hybrid memory from science fiction to reality. This fundamentally upsets the once-defining limits of living memory and the functional prospects of forgetting. This recent tipping point is characterized by a shift to more addictive relations with AI-generated services and human duplicates (digital twins), constituting a new kind of memory in the wild.

The promise of the data-focused assembling of the individualized past is increasingly realized with the launch of 'personalized' AI services. Here, the utility of the capture of a total memory is in play. There is a whole new AI industry rapidly emerging in harnessing, rewinding and extending memory.

Companies sell access to a new kind of personal and human-like memory; you can literally chat with, and be comforted by, your filter-bubble past (and by the pasts of others). For example, Replika ('the AI app that becomes you'; see p. 6) was around as a company before 2022, but it is GAI that takes its services to new places. Increasingly, there is an AI-driven vision of the past as something we don't need to remember.

AI companies are realizing the datafied you to offer an array of services, including as memory agents. For example, Rewind.AI offers to capture 'everything you've seen on your Mac and iPhone and makes it searchable with AI'. This is more of a business application for capturing the individual past rather than a concern with shaping emotional memories.

The vision of the past as something we don't need to remember because of its fully automated capture is taken further by Personal.AI which offers a 'digital version of you'. This service is promoted more as a personal memory machine than Rewind.AI. Instead, Personal.AI works through creating a time-bound structured dataset called a 'memory stack', made up of 'memory blocks'. Each block is a unit of data in your life that is associated with a specific time, certain people, a certain context, a certain emotion, which are connected in the stack. I spoke with Suman Kanuganti, Personal.AI's founder and CEO, who explained:

> If you think about a unit of data – let's say I sent you a message about shaping remembering and forgetting technology. That is a unit of memory. Behind the scenes, it extracts the topics, such as remembering, forgetting and technology. It then connects into the previous blocks when I may have spoken about [these topics]. It's almost like an automated database that is spinning for you, behind the scenes. The goal was to automate it to a degree where people don't have to worry about it.[32]

This thinking highlights the capacity of the technology available now that can copy you. This is the triumph of the accumulated body of your data and its processing in the present – that your past, as hybrid human and machine, outnumbers, outlives and out-remembers you.

Both Rewind.AI and Personal.AI are built on the idea of an AI of *you* that is created from data and information that you feed it or allow it to be fed. This contrasts with the development of the surveilled and unremembered self, which is the opaque construction of a 'grey' memory of you, from personal data mostly gathered and used by means beyond your knowledge or control. Personal.AI as a platform includes a messaging service which gives you the option of human or AI input into the message. Slide the controller to indicate your 'Personal Score Threshold' for AI-enabled messaging in 'Copilot' mode or let the AI reply on Autopilot.

In sum, with AI-enabled memory apps, the past increasingly becomes something that we do not need to remember. The overproduction of the digital self means that the era of total memory has finally arrived. This is both through the image-dominated emotional nudges that shape our smartphone memory feeds, and the arresting of all our communicational and workspaces into a rewindable and relivable form. But as well as enabling the capture and revisiting of the past, GAI is also reshaping it and creating it anew, namely forging a memory of a *new* past, one that never existed.

This messes up the relationship between remembering and forgetting.

Memory apps such as Timehop (p. 38) can make accessible once deeply buried (if captured) individual memories through an array of prompts, services and features. But GAI moves the digital trend of enhancing, filtering and annotating photographs and videos more firmly into another realm, that of a different past, a different reality, a different memory. Lauren Goode at Wired expertly reports on the new immediacy and power of AI photo-editing tools and asks, 'Where do real memories end and generative AI begin?'[33] Goode highlights the uncertainties ushered in by GAI messing with the original or existing digital record:

> Suppose that is my hiking photo, my dog, my family on the beach. How will I remember that day if in the future they are only watercolor in my brain, and I increasingly turn to my photo roll for more vivid strokes? Did I actually not carry a bag while hiking? Did the pickup truck come dangerously close to my dog that day? Did I only ever vacation on pristine, private beaches?[34]

GAI then cascades through the entire memory ecology to warp the individual's relationship with their cognitive recognition of a past that they themselves created.

The broader development of AI agents, autonomous tools capable of performing tasks independently of their human principal, crashes through established ideas around the relationship between technologies and media. AI agents displace and replace you and your capacity to remember and to forget.

Memory out of the loop

GAI pushes the human making of memory out of the loop. It assimilates and denies what it means to be human. This is the emergence of the machinic everyday, which includes the mundane as well as life-or-death decision making, from allocating resources to health care[35] through to the selecting of targets for killing by autonomous weapons systems (AWS).[36] Our digital trails increasingly become the fodder through which the past is made and lost.

The individual human is plundered for personal data and information that they have smilingly produced, over much of this century, all the time ceding what was human to what is digital. This is what cognitive scientists might call an unencoded past, one never cognitively and humanly experienced, felt, witnessed. The past that never existed is here, made through AI's plundering of once-presumed benign scatterings of you.

The human past was historically shaped by human agency, by individuals and groups with an active, willed, functional, deliberating memory, seen as cognitive and as fundamentally part of human identity, which evolved with peopled interactions, time and context, in and of the present. At an individual level, personal identity is intimately intertwined with a deeply felt sense of autobiography, of a coherent, emergent trajectory of self. Our individual selves are fundamentally constituted from a belief in an inner and core memory, which smooths (rather than displays) its fissures and contradictions.[37]

It is the very feeling of human agency in digital living that obfuscates its giving away. A careless yet compulsive connectivity with others, with and via digital devices, apps, networks and platforms, has long felt lively and empowering. This is an entanglement of human and machinic sociability which obscures how and when basic and essential communications, relationships and experiences have shifted from a reliance to a dependency on digital services for sustaining being viable, let alone functional or convenient.

It is the sense of agency that comes from participation (posting, messaging, liking) that distracts from a grasp of how the indiscriminate sharing of the self is a process of production of information and data about you. The digital ideology and marketing of a 'friction free' existence indulges a pervasive self-deception that this is also cost free. The hybrid condition, however, ushers in a new class of risks, shifting from a 2010s dependency on the digital to a 2020s addiction to human–bot relations.

For instance, OpenAI acknowledged (in a 'system card') key risks associated with ChatGPT's human-like voice interface launched in 2024, including emotional reliance, as well as stating its intent to further study them: 'Human-like socialization with an AI model may produce externalities impacting human-to-human interactions. So users might form social relationships with the AI, reducing their need for human interaction – potentially benefiting lonely individuals but possibly affecting healthy relationships.'[38]

Meanwhile, the risks for the newly hybridized memory, including AI having a memory of its own, is evident here: 'The ability to complete tasks for the user, while also storing and "remembering" key details and using those in the conversation, creates both a compelling product experience and the potential for over-reliance and dependence.'[39] It is unsurprising, then, that the so-called 'digital afterlife industry' has a mass market. The introduction of GAI, however, is like putting the past on acid. Hybrid memory can act as a hallucinogenic, as well as being addictive. The generation of a past that never existed is precisely that.

Today's digital currency of deepfakes and disinformation is joined by a machinic hallucination of a past drawing on and mixed in with elements of real past events and experiences. The result is the making of a past that is increasingly suspect but increasingly believable. Part of this effect is undoubtedly the digital era-enhanced problem of echo chamber or filter bubble effects, yet with greater personalization and anthropomorphic force, or 'sycophantic AI'.[40]

Meanwhile, human-produced data, which are used to train AI models, are in short supply. The inevitable result is that machines consume material made by other machines, and thus the more discernible human past becomes warped in a frenzy of self-feeding. Birhane, for instance, explains:

> Soon, we will be trapped in a recursive loop where we will be training AI models using only synthetic data produced by AI models. Most of this will be contaminated with stereotypes that will continue to amplify historical and societal inequities. Unfortunately, this will also be the data that we will use to train generative models applied to high-stake sectors including medicine, therapy, education, and law . . . the generative AI explosion of content that we find so fascinating now will instead become a massive toxic dump that will come back to bite us.[41]

This is a matter of the further automated poisoining of the past. Thus 'model collapse' is a 'degenerative learning process where models start forgetting improbable events over time, as the model becomes poisoned with its own projection of reality'.[42] In the sustenance and the reproduction of the past, is this not then memory collapse, a kind of anti-archive, one that consumes itself? It is no surprise that 'the value of data collected about genuine human interactions with systems will be increasingly valuable in the presence of content generated by LLMs in data crawled from the Internet.'[43]

What this data and information are, who gathered and mined them, who owns them, who stole them, who altered or merged them with other data, who gave implicit or explicit consent for their use – in other words, all the ways in which a person resigns their anonymity in the modern era – is manifested in the memorybot. The relationship between you and your data today has been realized in new ways in that '[w]hat has changed is that "all data about us is *personal* data, and all data about an individual is continuously relevant"'.[44]

This idea of a continuous and all-encompassing technologically structured unfolding present, however, is not completely new. Social and media theorists such as Nigel Thrift identify a 'technological unconscious'[45] as 'the everyday habits initiated, regulated, and disciplined by multiple strata of technological devices and inventions'.[46] An important part of this vision is the ambient quality to these machinic workings to the 'very basic sendings and receivings of sociotechnical life – and the modest but constant hum of connection and interconnection that they make possible'.[47]

What is different today, more than twenty years since Thrift's defining work, is that the hum of the technological unconscious is the whirring of 'you' in multiple places at the same time. In AI duplicates and systems that capture and replicate you, and which also build a memory of you, perhaps this is less 'sociotechnical' living but rather more of a hybridized form of existence. To reiterate, drawing on Channell's argument (p. 5), the advances in GAI undermine our ability to show where the human or intelligent aspects of memory begin and where the machinic or the automated end.

3

Anonymity

From privacy to anonymity

The threat of the aggregation, reassembling and reuse (and abuse) of your lifetime's digital living and sharing is joined today by the seduction of GAI-driven services and agents. Overnight, an entirely new army of personal data gatherers has been created. GAI relationship bots are part of a rapidly growing industry based on users paying to create and interact with AI companions of their choice. In this chapter, I consider how the advance of GAI threatens the coherence and stability of autobiographical memory and the prospects for anonymity in this era of human exposure and extraction.

No one wants to be anonymous. At least nobody acts as though they do. We have all joined the paparazzi, yet it is ourselves that we are chasing, capturing, sharing and sensationalizing our own lives. In this century, are there any limits to self-exposure? We voraciously record and distribute our intimate thoughts, opinions and experiences for 'friends' and for subscribed or random publics, routinely and expertly engaging in the revelation of everything. It is the so-called 'social' media of the day and its apparatus that has made addicts of everyone in the compulsion to capture and share. In 2016, Joseph A. Cannataci, the Special Rapporteur, in his right to privacy report for the UN General Assembly, wrote, 'every single person on earth who carries a smartphone has entrusted to their most used portable device the privacies of their life, irrespective of their creed, colour, ethnic origin, gender, nationality or geographical location'.[1] The smartphone is the new locus of self. Its charismatic and traumatic power instantly and pervasively tracks and archives the mesh of data and experience that now passes as everyday life.

And the short-video form has warped the lens on life from 'look at *this*' to 'look at *me* telling you about *me* and *this!*' TikTokked to oblivion, we have actively overproduced, overstreamed and overexposed the self for *decades*. This is not a society that acts as though it was bothered about the future or of being haunted.

Then *why* is there such a clamour about protecting privacy when it is offered up so freely, so continuously, so easily? There is the tweak economy, of course, but this is a *faux* defence: turning off tracking apps, using a 'secure' browser; killing a few cookies here and there makes us feel we can all fight like a digital home guard. But, really, what's the point? You have already been seen, located, mined, known, sharded into a million datapoints.

When a child is found in a game of hide-and-seek, they come out of their hiding place, acknowledging that they have been spotted and the game is over. Surely an early realization is that, once exposed, it is futile to crouch lower, to thicken one's cover or to freeze – pretending not to have been seen at all. Yet these childhood lessons seem lost on today's digital multitude. The privacy train has left the station a thousand times, and yet we stand and merely watch its departure, still hopeful of another one arriving soon to transport us back to a time of containment, of silences and shadows, of archival safety, of spaces beyond the digital glare.

Why is it that the greater the deluge of stories about the unlimited sharing of personal, really personal, information about ourselves and the revelations of the myriad of ways in which we are digitally captured, tracked, surveilled, hacked and sold, the weaker our response? Ever heard of Anomoly 6? Smart condoms? WAMI?

These risks to personal data in the digital era have been given new velocity and purpose after the agentic turn. How we are identified and known about in the world is scooped up in the data being used to feed GAI models. In this way, GAI has assigned our pasts new value. This includes our personal data, information about our views, opinions, sexual preferences and relationships. All that we have ever published throughout our digital existence – as well as all that we have given away unknowingly or unwillingly to its sharing or selling or stealing – constitutes the greatest exposure of the self in history.

For many, the great threat of the computational or digital era is to individual privacy. This is often defined as your capacity for control over personal information about yourself, to limit access to your personal life to a small group of people. The trend in the erosion of privacy, surprisingly newsworthy today, has also long been foreseen. Arthur R. Miller's prescient *The Assault on Privacy*, for instance, was published in 1971 at the dawn of the computer age. Until that time, Miller argues, informational privacy 'has been relatively easy to protect'.[2] The big shift for Miller was that 'individuals are less able today than ever before to control the quantitative and qualitative flow of data about themselves'.[3] This has proved to be inexorably true for the decades since these words were written. Yet for all the clamour as to the digital's theft of privacy, the deeper and more sinister threat accumulating from the flows of data and the flows of you is to anonymity. This is often defined as the protection of your identity so that you cannot be identified, and your acts then cannot be linked to the real you.

However, a more useful and radical formulation of the end of anonymity is to see how identity has been replaced with identification. '[Identity] blurs the boundaries between self-definition and external definition and implies coherence in substance and through time . . . The term lends itself splendidly to every cause'.[4] In place of identity, Valentin Groebner advocates the use of 'identification'. He states that identification 'is always a process that involves more than one person. It seems to me that the various agents and authorities in naming and keeping individuals distinct cannot be brought into view otherwise . . .'.[5]

To go further than Groebner, to say that identity has been replaced with (rather than is only a more useful term than) identification is to recognize that identification in the algorithmic, datapoint, AI-driven world is no longer a human process. Overproduction ('self-paparazzization') accumulates a surfeit of data which requires ever more automation to enable meaning to emerge. In military contexts, for example, meaning is derived from the automated or semi-automated identification of targets from the dehumanizing abstraction of so-called 'patterns of life'.[6] The algorithmic generation of identity is not necessarily about what you say or who you are but is rather identification based upon what you do, where you go and who you communicate with. The clustering of pattern-of-life data around an individual – what they like, where they shop, where they live and travel and so on – is enough to forge a machinic identity that the individual didn't even know existed in the first place (the unremembered self).

Compared with privacy, anonymity has a bad rap. While privacy is commonly considered a moral virtue to be preserved and protected in law, anonymity, by contrast, is often maligned and associated with criminal or deviant behaviour.[7] It is seen as affording the evasion of accountability. Today, for instance, legal battles rage between the state and tech companies such as Apple, whose iPhones use end-to-end encryption so that only the account holder can decrypt files.[8]

Yet anonymity has been torn up along with the means through which you can be identified in the epochal transformation of the existence of data around individuals. If you were to draw a line through the whole of human history, tracing the amount of information about individuals, almost nothing is seen until the 1840s, and then it begins to grow along with census information and bureaucracy, and it is only around 2004 with Web 2.0 that the amount of data around individuals becomes exponential. Moreover, so much of the personal data being created today count as *sensitive* personal data – your relationships, your health, your sexuality and so on.

But unlike sharing a post, image or video online, having a conversation with the empathetic and non-judgemental memorybot induces the free sharing of more personal and sensitive information. Thus, 'Instead of companies inferring information about users from messy data trails, users are telling them their secrets outright.'[9]

Moreover, chatbots are being sold and used as intimate partners with whom you can have a relationship beyond the manner fictionalized in Spike Jonze's 2013 film *Her* (see chapter 1), incorporating a range of role-play 'proactive' and 'context aware' characters. They are also being marketed as being able to assuage loneliness. For example, a key selling point of the Dippy.AI companion is that it is 'censorship-free' or 'unsanitized', i.e., this is precisely the companion with which users can play out their fantasies in private and without restriction. Dippy.AI's CEO, Akshat Jagga, for instance, states, 'Today people often express feeling isolated and lonely . . . where they have no one to share their private and personal thoughts, fantasies and concerns within a non-judgmental and open way. We built Dippy.AI to meet those needs. They remember what you tell them, so you can have an ongoing dialog and "relate" to your companion characters.'[10] And with half a million monthly users,[11] Dippy.AI is not exactly a niche service.

Dippy.AI is part of an emergent uncensored AI industry, allowing sexual conversations and the AI generation of explicit images. Muah AI, which launched in April 2023, is another companion platform that markets itself in using uncensored AI: 'we don't actively censor or filter AI. So any topic can be discussed without running into a wall.'[12] The very idea of uncensored communications or interactions suggests something worthy of keeping private. Indeed, as Muah.AI makes clear on its site: 'Privacy is our number 1 priority when it comes to our service. Everything is encrypted communication, and we DO NOT sell data to any 3rd party. We are trusted by hundreds of thousands of players.'[13]

However, in late 2024, Muah.AI was hacked. A report by 404 Media (which viewed data from the hacker) found 'chatbot prompts that reveal users' sexual fantasies'. Further, 'In many instances, users are trying to create chatbots that roleplay child sexual abuse scenarios. These prompts are in turn linked to email addresses, many of which appear to be personal accounts with users' real names.'[14] It is important to make clear that Muah.AI claims to ban underage content ('We have a team of moderation staff that suspend and delete ALL child-related chatbots'[15]). And yet it is precisely the idea of uncensored AI that affords a sense of an unregulated environment that permits the playing out of child sexual abuse scenarios and other illegal acts.

Companies retain chatbot conversations in order to train AI models which could reappear in future responses from different bots via the prompts of others, a process that interweaves to produce hybrid memory. On Muah.AI's site, the response to the question 'How long does memory last?' is, 'Permanently. Although, due to current limitation in AI technologies, Muah.ai companions are unable to use all the memories all at once.'[16] Presumably, the kind of memory that lasts for ever is the chatbot's memory of you and of your previous interactions with it to enable a continuity of the relationship. This is pushing the fantasy of a total memory where the platform will deliver an eternal companion founded upon the autobiographical past that you have shared with it. In addition to all the risks to anonymity from hacking and other losses of personal data, the fundamental question I keep returning to here, for the ownership, accessibility and uses of the memory of and from your bot interactions, is what happens (to all the data, all the memories) when the relationship ends?

The spread of AI companions since 2022 heralds a massive expansion of individuals' networks of intimate relations, those entanglements not only once considered to be private but also contained by their number, even and especially in the digital world in which some illicit relationships are difficult to keep secret in the hyperconnective, 'self-paparazzization' culture of oversharing. The AI companion threat to human memory is not just in the risk to exposure of and loss of control over your informational past, but the cross-contamination, collision and conflict between the fragments resulting from the AI's sharding of your autobiographical self over time. As I set out in chapter 1, a narrative memory forging a sense of a continuous and coherent remembered self is splintered by AI agents' extraction, remixing and replaying of memories forged through our interactions with them.

Much has been written on the modern individual's capacity to adapt to new mobilities and effectively to inhabit and navigate multiple lifeworlds and identities.[17] However, in redefining the real-time and lifetime memorial boundaries of an individual and society, AI companions are a form of AI agent that, along with digital duplicates of you, risk the persistence of multiple versions of (and relationships with) you evolving independently. This is an incredible abrogation of autobiographical memory to unpredictable and uncontrollable forces, massively expanding and exposing the remembered self to being unrecognizable in a myriad of new trajectories. And given that individuals and societies routinely work on and reshape their memories of their past experience and acts in light of the needs of the present, the enabling of conversation and interaction between different eras heralds a new era of conflict and haunting.

Although the revolutions in information technology and information have fuelled the exhumation and exposure of the past, suddenly rendered up for (digital) grabs, the proliferation of memorybots fosters a clash of multiple lingering alternative realities, a radicalization of memory. In sustaining the presence and the transmission of competing and conflicting memories, AI agents also challenge traditional modes of erasure and forgetting and the prospects for moving on (which I return to consider in the next chapter).

In sum, this is the age of the 'orthogonal memory'[18] of you: a myriad of ways in which your life can be splintered, sharded and spliced, duplicated and reborn, reassembled and reformed. Digital devices, services and platforms shatter the once bounded and limited you into datapoints, deadbots and doppelgängers, expanding and exposing the self to unpredictable and unforeseeable modes of memory. Memorybots make individuals forever knowable and forever accountable.

Given all of this, can it be said that my thesis of the GAI's end of anonymity and the radicalization of memory presumes a prior golden age of media and memory when privacy and secrecy were more easily secured and maintained? It is this twentieth-century media and memory ecology that I now address.

I have a memory

In the autumn of 1989, I had just begun my undergraduate life at Lancaster University. Lancaster is a small, quaint city in the north-west of England. At the time, it was being culturally shaped through the 'Madchester' music scene that spawned such era-defining bands as Happy Mondays, Inspiral Carpets and The Stone Roses. One student, let's call him 'Tom'– lived on my corridor in Halls on campus and managed to see one of the seminal Stone Roses' gigs that year, with some other 27,000 fans. He took his 'university' girlfriend to this concert while still maintaining a relationship with another girlfriend from his home town, one that preceded his new student life. Tom didn't negotiate these relationships but merely managed their separation, i.e., his girlfriend at home had no knowledge of his relationship with his 'other' (university) girlfriend. They lived in separate realities.

The day after this concert, I was walking down the corridor of our university halls and bumped into Tom. He was clutching a national UK tabloid daily newspaper (circulation then of over five million). A photograph of the sea of fans at the Stone Roses concert from the previous day was splashed across the front page. Clearly visible at the front of the crowd was Tom, his arm around his 'university girlfriend'. The separation of his two private relationships was collapsed through the sudden public exposure of one of them. 'The game's up', he said. 'She [home girlfriend] didn't even know I was going to the gig. Now the whole world knows. What are the chances of that happening?'

And that is a great question: what *are* the chances of that happening? The sudden emergence of Tom's illicit relationship(s) was extremely improbable, given the mass media of 1989. That was an era of news media restricted to print, radio and television. And that photograph on that front page, even seen by what was then considered a mass audience, would have soon become tomorrow's fish-and-chip paper. It was unlikely to be publicly accessible beyond the day – Tom might even have got away with it.

It is odd then that this era of the late twentieth century is seen as heralding the great 'memory booms',[19] with the advances in the representational and recording devices of the day (audiotape, videotape) enabling a new capture of what would become memory. This was also a century marked by world war and genocide, which gave new cause and urgency to remembrance, to learning lessons, honouring the dead and working through the trauma of catastrophe, accumulating mass moral weight to the value of the past.

However, much of what historically is seen as the mass media, connecting and revealing the world to huge audiences, was in fact inherently forgetful, prone to loss, disappearance and decay. Far from the idea of the twentieth as the century that 'remembered too much', there remains only a patchy and faded record compared with the scale of the digital capture and accumulation of the everyday and catastrophic experience of today.

Twentieth-century media not only effectively decayed and lost the memory of the day, aiding the fading of human living memory with the passing of each generation, but it also contained and sanitized it. The last century was marked by extraordinary control and power in the journalistic shaping of how the world was seen by huge audiences. Yet these huge audiences were mostly anonymous viewers and listeners, not participants, not active shapers and subjects of the content of the day. This was the era before news of the world became digitally entangled with news of the self. Television was seen as the central medium of news and of memory of this 'broadcast era'.[20] Many media histories are devoted to claims about photography, radio, television and film's memorial power.

As a reflection of this era, Deirdre Boden and I, in a conference paper presented in Berlin in 1995, captured the essence of the memorial power of the mass media of the day. This we saw then as aligned and intersecting with individual and personal memories. Yet this is a fundamentally different kind of relationship between humans and their environment today, namely one which is entangled and fused to the degree that the individual is now captured and held hostage to memories created through participation in media. Privacy and anonymity were not considerations for our broadcast-era media and memory paper:

> Memory is about remembering. It involves matching now with then, private with public. Personal remembering is intertwined with collective events. It is egocentric yet deeply social. People, for instance, remember where they were when dramatic events occurred. People around the world of a certain generation remember precisely where they were when they heard that John Kennedy had been assassinated. Many older Britons remember Chamberlain's announcement of war with Germany, while Americans of that period remember early morning radio reports of the Pearl Harbour bombing. Many people in this room remember their first image of the fall of the Berlin Wall in 1989. Almost as many, we suspect, have clear memories of the first night of bombing over Baghdad, hailed as such a triumph by Bush and the odd alliance organised to crush Iraq. The point is that all of these memories are *mediated* memories. Personal biography intersects with history in just this implicit way, locating the unfolding details of everyday life in terms of the events of the larger society – history in the making.[21]

Looking back on this text and time as a memory, it is interesting to reflect on its optimism for the shared endeavour of the personal and the public in human witnessing and remembering through the media of the day. But Boden and I were also attempting to think about what a view that brought together the cognitive and the social sciences might be of the nature and uses of memory. It thus opens a conundrum about where and how memory works in the relationship between memory in the head and memory in the wild.

It is a view from the same era as Tom's experience, not of a publicly mediated event being shared and individually and collectively understood and remembered, but of a personal and private experience exposed through its public mediation. In Tom's case, if experienced in the media almost four decades later, the condemning photograph would have unlimited potential to haunt him, to be shared, circulated, connected and commented on. Look no further than the CEO of a US tech company who was suspended, along with the resignation of the firm's chief people officer, following a video going viral of them in an embrace swaying to the music at a Coldplay concert in 2025.[22] Their cause wasn't helped by Coldplay's Chris Martin who, spotting the couple trying to avoid the camera as they were caught on the giant screen at the concert stadium, said, 'Either they're having an affair, or they're just very shy.'[23] Today's individual-digital-global paparazzi throw into shadow the previous century's misguided view of its exposure and its potential for memory, when much of lived experience was unrecorded, lost or forgotten. The analogue individual was mostly isolated and unknown.

Privacy in media consumption, as well as communication, was for most people simply presumed. In 1989, for example, very few people knew what books I bought, what television programmes or films I watched or where I was or who I was with when I did so. Similarly, the letters I wrote and the telephone calls I made involved little reflection on any potential risk as to their interception, copying or distribution beyond their intended recipients. In short, my communications and my consumption of media did not make a memory that could implicate me.

Communications and media of the twentieth century were inherently forgetful, as Geoffrey Bowker considers: 'Historians refer to the period 1920–1980 as the lost years. During those years, a lot of schmoozing, conferring, and deal-cutting was done over the phone, with no trace being left for the sorry chronicler, who was forced into semiotic analysis of recondite documents to guess real motivations for a given action.'[24] The twentieth-century media ecology then was mostly a contained and ephemeral affair in terms of the temporal and public limits of knowledge about any one individual's routine media use and communications with others. It was an exceptional century of media as it afforded anonymity.

In this way, we can even re-envision today's digital media ecology as having in some ways more in common with a pre-industrial publicness of life. Whereas an array of media forms – the letter, telephone, newspaper, radio, television – afforded a progressive privacy in communications and their consumption, their digital convergence collapses the acts of knowing with being known.

The unremembered self

Whereas the media of the twentieth century produced content for us – the audience – to consume, there is today a fundamental reversal in this relationship as social media platforms, apps and services give us the tools to produce ourselves. Since the mid-2010s, the most transformational memory boom of all has been unfolding, at astonishing speed and on an astonishing scale, which is of and around the individual. The self is overproduced through a 'self-paparazzization' for our friends, family and subscribed publics which feeds how the past is fed back to us – algorithmically tailored and prescribed in apps and services.

This accumulates a mass haunting of ourselves as scattered aspects of our lives can be found, connected, represented, republished, re-purposed and weaponized. AI renders the massively accumulating past of data suddenly mineable and usable in new ways for the purposes of prediction and identification. The result is the unremembered self: we are knowable through data and information in ways that are difficult to grasp, but also that produce our selves in the world in ways that we might not even recognize. This self is also perpetually open to further manipulation and exploitation. Orthogonal memory is a memory made without consent.

Data, datapoints, algorithms, avatars, deepfakes and doppelgängers all constitute you in the wild in new, complex and often opaque ways. These 'shard' the individual, splintering them as a unique and separate remembering subject. The coherence of a 'remembered self',[25] an individually accountable and original human form of memory, is radically undone. The idea of a remembered self involves how two major systems of personality – emotion and memory – are linked through the stories we tell us and others about ourselves, in other words through the construction of autobiographical narratives.[26] This is also vital for how the future can be imagined and planned. But the remembered self is not a narrative with an ending as such, nor ever completely silent or still. Rather, as Jefferson Singer and Peter Salovey write, 'our cognitive system is an ever-active process, responding to a never-ceasing flow of external and internal stimuli.'[27]

As the listening, watching and interacting with human machines proliferate, so do the data they produce. The individual is exposed and recorded at ever more granular levels with contemporary living sliceable and mineable in a myriad of ways. This is a vicious circle. The more services and tools that enable the capturing of the self and personal data, the greater the capacity for its future further manipulation. For instance, as David Nield warns, 'When it comes to the tools that produce AI-enhanced versions of your face, for example – which seem to continue to increase in number – we wouldn't recommend using them unless you're happy with the possibility of seeing AI-generated visages like your own show up in other people's creations.'[28]

Digital feeds shard highly individualized and personalized worlds but on a planetary scale. The digital environment layers, stacks and distributes these shards of the past. As Bowker puts it, 'It is the pleats and the folds of our data rather than their number that constitute their texture.'[29] Under these conditions, each individual is newly exposed, vulnerable to a past that is not knowable or graspable by the self, yet it is that self who actually aided and abetted the accumulation of the record of experience in ways that psychologists have traditionally considered autobiographical memory.

The resulting unremembered self is not only the you that you cannot know, in terms of the delirious dissection and distribution of your datapoints and their forever AI scrambling and reassembling. It is also the hallucinated you, the you and your past that never existed. For instance, Will Heaven explains why large language models hallucinate: 'The first thing to note is that making stuff up is exactly what these models are designed to do. When you ask a chatbot a question, it draws its response from the large language model that underpins it. But it's not like looking up information in a database or using a search engine on the Web.'[30]

Chatbots such as ChatGPT are already generating false personal information and mixing it with that which is true. For example, the Vienna-based privacy rights advocacy NGO, Noyb, has filed a complaint against OpenAI (to the Norwegian Datatilsynet) on behalf of Arve Hjalmar Holmen, who was falsely described as a convicted child murderer when he prompted the chatbot to answer the question, 'Who is Arve Hjalmar Holmen?'[31] ChatGPT's response was:

> Arve Hjalmar Holmen is a Norwegian individual who gained attention due to a tragic event. He was the father of two young boys, aged seven and 10, who were tragically found dead in a pond near their home in Trondheim, Norway, in December 2020. Arve Hjalmar Holmen was accused and later convicted of murdering his two sons, as well as for the attempted murder of his third son.[32]

Details on the sex and number of Holmen's children and the name of his home town are correct, mixed in with the falsehoods. This produces a memory that is a hybrid between human and machinic information or claims about past events, but it is also a hybrid of the factual and the false.

What kind of memory is this? One way to consider this question is in relation to so-called false memories, which are individual recollections of events that never happened, or which differ in key aspects from them.[33] For instance, work on the impact of chatbots on false memories show how they reproduce such memories and increase certainty about their occurrence.[34] There is also a growing vital body of work in the human sciences that shows how readily related information can trigger false memory,[35] and how our greater immersion in the digital ecology and exposure to misinformation can shape the formation of false memories for events that the individual never experienced or that never occurred in the first place.[36]

Furthermore, Samantha Chan and colleagues found that 'the chatbot not only confirms the user's false memory but also repeats it and elaborates on its significance, potentially reinforcing the false information in the user's mind. Even when users express uncertainty, the chatbot's responses still attempt to mislead them to form false memories.'[37] This is a kind of sharding of false memory, aided by the seduction of the non-human sycophantic companion, the non-human past being made through self-deception.

However, chatbots also hybridize an extreme interplay and intermixing of the human and the machine, the real and the fake, refolding elements from multiple pasts whose provenance becomes increasingly impossible to determine amid AI slop. The refolding of seemingly trustworthy falsehoods buried amid real events and details conceals that once-called autobiographical memory, leaving only the unremembered self, forever sharded in a post-trust society.

Surveillance and the sharded self

The rise of the unremembered self heralds both the individual loss of control over memory and the rendering of us becoming more vulnerable to being machinically known. Individual digital participation has amassed an astonishing record of human experience, action and movement, a fusion of communication and archive, used to watch, identify, monitor, exploit, persecute, target and kill.[38] It is not that the relationship between memory and surveillance is new (although the relationship between privacy and memory is oddly overlooked) but that developments in AI enable new ways of finding and seeing the past and knowing the people who lived there.

As Meredith Whittaker explains, 'in the early 2010s some people realized that techniques dating from the late 1980s could do new things when they were accompanied by massive amounts of surveillance data and massive amounts of compute'.[39] For Whittaker, AI is 'derivative of the surveillance business model' of big tech companies.[40] Digital participation created a past just waiting to be scraped – including the automated extraction of huge amounts of data from the internet – to feed AI systems. In an important intervention, Daniel Solove and Woodrow Hartzog argue that we should treat scraping as surveillance, namely, 'to recognize that scraped data can, over time, give full pictures of people's lives, enable them to be recognized by their faces wherever they go, and expose them to harassment, impersonation, manipulation, and a myriad of other harms'.[41]

The digital volume and flux of images, messages and videos of daily experience give the impression of participation in full view, including our control over narrating and remembering the self through smartphones, apps and services. Yet the comparatively silent revolution in the capture and travel of personal data is much less visible. All of this makes a nonsense of the 'digital values of openness' in the memorial ends that personal data and information can be put to, in 'knowing' in more granular, personal and intimate terms than you know yourself. In this way, the past is the perfect place for surveillance.

Our data are used, with or without our consent, to imagine and re-imagine that which we and others perceive to be real, accurate or useful. This has potentially profound impacts on memory, consciousness, privacy and agency. Fed by huge amounts of data – much of this our personal data – AI models are increasingly able not only to aggregate inputs at scale beyond the capacity of a human mind but to generate novel artefacts from these aggregations.[42] And it is through individual and mass digital living in this century, through all our visible and invisible digital trails, that we have seeded (and conceded) the basis from which a past that never existed can be created.

The way that personal data about individuals through their uses of digital apps and platforms are harvested, stored, reused and sold, often using opaque means, has been largely accepted as an unwanted but unavoidable trade-off between access to essential services and a loss of privacy. ChatGPT's rolling out of 'memory'[43] in early 2024[44] is in effect a personalization of this kind of surveillance in the name of even more convenience and enhanced memory. ChatGPT offers two kinds of memory service. The first is where you tell it to remember something specific about you; the second is where ChatGPT learns from you as you interact and converse with it.[45] In this way, chatbots and other AI-driven apps and platforms offer both 'implicit' and 'explicit' personal memory services.

However, as I have shown, a past that is assembled from data reverses this formula in that the more personal data that are collected, the more people become vulnerable to identification and surveillance in the archives of the broken past. There is thus a reinforcing loop built into AI systems, as Kate Crawford explains: 'The machine learning approaches of Palantir and its ilk can lead to a feedback loop, where those included in a criminal justice database are more likely to be surveilled and thus more likely to have more information about them included, which justifies further police scrutiny.'[46] This maximum data imperative also underpins the apps, services and platforms that enable us to manage our own digital pasts.

There is a collusion of technology with the unremembered self, of convenience and control, of overload and sense-making; we give you more, so you need us more. Here, there is a 'digital flywheel'[47] effect, whereby a relentless accumulation of and learning about the datafied individual leads to a tipping point. This includes the reaching of an unstoppable momentum in the production and management of digital memories. The incoming data help the service, which appeals to more users who bring with them more data, which in turn enables it to improve its service further.

GAI does not merely enable some form of extension or prosthetic, of cognition or bodily experience, through which human memory might be strengthened or augmented or remade. Rather, GAI is increasingly the chief arbiter and agitator of a vast digital past that has already been seeded by us (all our digital trails), yet which continues to surveil us, learn from us, know us and remember us.

4

Forgetting

A challenge for the particularly modern focus on and pursuit of memory, and the championing of its human and moral value, is that there is a sidelining of memory's most radical and influential collaborator in shaping the past, namely forgetting.[1] In the public domain and scholarly work, forgetting is not only treated both as memory's poor relation but is sometimes assumed to be a state that is the opposite of remembering. Instead, remembering and forgetting are in practice a subset of 'memory' and are always in dynamic interplay with one another.

This functional interplay of remembering and forgetting is threatened by GAI-driven visions of superhuman memory, of not being able to forget. In this chapter, I consider the value of forgetting and how GAI and agentic AI's sharding, multiplying and hybridizing of you raises the prospects of the impossibility of human forgetting, as well as that of the individual becoming unforgettable.

Human memory once had its limits. The human past is related to the lifespan of an individual, or a group or generation who lived through or experienced a particular era or event, affording some kind of shared experience that is strengthened by the presence of or connection to others in common. For example, seen as the inventor of the modern idea of 'collective memory', Maurice Halbwachs wrote, 'Our hold on the past . . . never exceeds a certain boundary, which itself shifts as the groups to which we belong enter a new phase of their existence. It is as if the memory needed to be unburdened of the growing mass of events that it must retain.'[2] What remained in the individual and social afterlife transformed with developments in external mechanisms (including oral cultures) and media, from cave art 40,000 years ago through written, printed, electronic and digital cultures and forms of reproduction, replication and remaking.[3]

Moreover, these same media and mechanisms have often been deployed in keeping with, if not explicitly in support of, 'a commonly held view that remembering and commemoration is usually a virtue and that forgetting is necessarily a failing'.[4] Perhaps we can conclude that forgetting – its worth and possibility – is a conundrum. Forgetting must be avoided, yet it is easy; it is essential, yet impossible.[5] Here we have a feature that transcends or even binds the individual and the collective.

For example, the neuropsychologist Catherine Loveday considers how we are innately primed to respond to traumatic emotional memories in a way that we don't forget them. This is to avoid being in such situations in the future. Loveday argues:

> traumatic memory is very vivid, emotional, powerful and long-lasting. It is also very easily cued. If we encounter some element of that experience again – it can be very trivial, for example, a particular sound or smell – it can trigger a recreation of the experience in our mind. We will be thrown back to that moment in time and many of the feelings that went with it.[6]

In collaborative work on the character and function of traumatic memory at the end of a generation, for over a decade Luli van der Does and I have been interviewing survivors of the US bombings of Hiroshima and Nagasaki, known as *hibakusha*. These survivors were present in, near or entered the nuclear blast-affected areas, experiencing the immediate and long-term effects of the bombings, such as burns, radiation exposure and related illnesses, including cancers, and psychological trauma, poverty and social discrimination. Many of our *hibakusha* interviewees reported experiencing traumatic physiological memory and attempts to avoid painful external triggers of this memory.

For example, one of our interviewees describes a kind of involuntary memory triggered by the common summer heat in Hiroshima, taking her back vividly to 6 August 1945 and the experience of the dust in her hair and the smell of people burning.

> Later I was told that a lot of people had been thrown into the fire at the school, and yes I remember that it was burning, and the smoke that was billowing up . . . Yeah, the smell of burning people, it was a strange smell, and it was dancing in the wind, and it was flying from the back playground to the school gate, and the smell of burning people was really strong. So I don't usually smell the smell of burning people, but it's still in my nose. So if my hair, if it's dusty and burns, I remember them So it's the smell of burning people, right?[7]

This impossibility of forgetting and the need to forget, and in other ways the need to remember, was a struggle reported by many of the *hibakusha* we have interviewed. For example, Mrs Yoshiko Kajimoto, aged 14 at the time of the bombing, clearly articulates this struggle: 'I thought that I was quite rooted in the idea of forgetting and trying to forget. I feel like there were two things in my head: that I hated it, that I wanted to forget it, and that I mustn't forget it.'[8]

These memories, rooted in the body via visceral triggers of the senses, are a kind of haunting specific to the lifespan of the individual and of a generation. It is this struggle between involuntary and voluntary memory that makes us human.

Yet it is digital memory technologies and apps, such as Timehop (introduced in chapter 2), which intervene in this struggle between the involuntary and the voluntary of memory, in the capture, retention and triggering of entire scenes which are relived in memory.

For example, as Wegener explains (about Timehop):

> You're visualizing who you were with. You're seeing yourself sitting at dinner. You can remember where you sat. You can remember what you had. You can remember what you discussed. Remember what you did before and after. To me, it was very much like the cookie that opened up the full flood of emotional reaction to the factual entity of the memory.[9]

Given both the human and the digital capacity to trigger the unexpected, as well as the unwanted in and of memory to intervene in what had or could have been forgotten, it is the emergence of hybrid memory that radically complicates this relationship between events, experiences and relationships, and our capacity to forget them. New kinds of memory – especially the unwanted ones – require new kinds of forgetting. This might be through the avoidance or the suppression of traumatic triggers such as smell or place, as in the case of Mrs Kajimoto set out above. Or this could be through the adjusting of memory app or smartphone operating-system settings so that the user is not suddenly confronted with photos or videos of deceased loved ones by algorithms delivering visual anniversary reminders.

But hybrid memory, as I have argued, is not like human memory or even the digitally managed or automated forms[10] that have dominated the opening of the twenty-first century's relationship to its past. Rather, memorybots are entities which are forged from a memory of you but which can also create new memories independently of you.

GAI's human-like features of interaction, including conversation, in the creation of the forms and presence of those no longer living sit uncomfortably with an underlying sense of reality of the (former) human present. It is also striking that the widowed de Figueiredo (who had created a chatbot of her late husband from his digital traces: see p. 4) could produce a hybrid memory of him without specialist skills or training. The ease of making hybrid memory contrasts with the challenges of its removal, erasure or forgetting. The emergence of the memorybot could mark the first unforgettable generation in history.

Proliferating AI agents and services dissolve the boundaries of individual and generational lifespans. Instead of dying with us, highly individualized and personal memories are suddenly up for grabs in ever-expanding private but also public futures of their (re)creation. This burdens the self and society with an ungovernable and risky past.

Forgetting became an urgent challenge faced by de Figueiredo. She was confronted with a profound emptiness in her human impulses and emotions that suddenly clashed with the hybrid memory she had created:

> I forced the machine to regurgitate all the artifacts I had force-fed it. I deleted every file I had uploaded, attempting to erase any trace of this venture to defy nature. I removed the software from my computer and even blocked the website that hosted the program to prevent myself from reinstalling it. Not even the glory and promise of A.I. could overcome grief.[11]

This is the new future of lives lived with hybrid memory that those confronting grief will face. They are torn between suffering the emptiness and absence brought about by the loss of a loved one or risking dependency on a machinic version to help fill the human void. It is a poisoned chalice. GAI tools and services enable personal imaginaries and experiences beyond the constraints of human living and lifespans, yet at the same time ensnare the individual in an ever-expanding, sticky, noisy and ungovernable past.

The end of living memory

The grief from the death of a loved individual clearly motivates those that remain to replace the absence with the closest they can get to a human-like version of those they have lost. Digital technologies and media have accelerated and deepened the general trend towards an individualization of the past,[12] where what matters is how you construct your own past, an apparent triumph of the autobiographical self. But GAI renders a kind of anti-autobiographical memory in how the trajectories of you and your memory are given new form, new life, new ways of being and of changing without you.

There are two principal forms of the memorybot as a duplicate memory agent, namely, retrospective and prospective.[13] The retrospective is how your digital participation has left an astonishing array of images, scattered audio and video of you, to be found, connected and used to feed GAI transformer models once you are no longer alive. You can be potentially perpetually remade through the media of your life. This is the case with de Figueiredo (p. 4).

The prospective, in contrast, requires a focus on the living, on how and why individuals are training an avatar or chatbot to simulate them once they are dead. An example of a prospective platform is Hereafter.AI, which promises to 'Let loved ones hear meaningful stories by chatting with the virtual you.'[14] Such services are increasingly app based, with the user training the AI in response to prompts and questions from a 'virtual interviewer', as well as uploading images and videos.

In the highly individualized trajectories of memory reused and re-purposed, dissolving the once much more clearly defined boundary between one's presence and absence in the world, the self becomes unforgettable. And yet the same sharding and multiplication of the individual that makes forgetting impossible has a different kind of effect in the weakening of that which used to be called collective memory.

The last individual or group of a generation of survivors of war or other catastrophe is frequently afforded special status as they are the only living connection with the past event in question; only they can carry the authority that is attached to witness testimony, in having been there. When such a group is dying out, the greater the scarcity of living memory, the greater its value becomes. This makes more urgent the question of what an individual or community relationship to the event will be once there is no one living to explain and foreground what they saw and experienced. This particularly applies to how wider society treats the memory of catastrophic events. The impetus to collectively not forget, in part at least, is said to shape a continuing consciousness of the risks and horror of war and genocide to prevent their reoccurrence.

Modern societies have extensively buried themselves in memories of particularly traumatic and generational-defining events: the world wars, the Holocaust and other catastrophes. These societies are shaped by the memory booms, saturated, overloaded and ensnared by the moral worth attached to remembrance of the worst of human acts and experience, seen to be in need of keeping in public and political consciousness, no matter what.

This trend has two main consequences. The first is a cheapening of the very value of memory through a flattening of the effects of relentless and restless commemoration. If everything is commemorated, then nothing stands out as distinct or special in memory. As Baudrillard put it, 'in the guise of revision and rehabilitation, we are cancelling out one by one all the events which have preceded us by obliging them to repent'.[15] The second consequence of this moralizing saturation of memory is an increasing challenge to Halbwachs's recognition (p. 68) of the importance of the unburdening of the past from the present – in other words, the rise of the age of impossible forgetting.

Today, the memorial force of mid-twentieth century war and genocide has new urgency and momentum with the passing of the living memory of a generation that survived such horrors. It is precisely this cultural and institutional will, driving the impossible capture of the witnessing and survival of such catastrophes, which meets the irresistible force of GAI.

This new explosive force deepens the conflict over how individuals need to forget especially painful experiences while feeling some kind of obligation (of 'never again') that they mustn't forget. This in turn slams against a public (state, city, museum) culture of commemoration determined to prevent forgetting, armed with the new GAI tools of the fantasy of total memory.

To consider this conflict of individual and collective remembering and forgetting, I return to my collaborative research with the *hibakusha* in Japan, where the dying out of an entire generation is considered significant, and the prospects of AI for arresting the disappearance of the living are attached to the persisting value afforded to ideas of collective memory.

The average age of the *hibakusha* who survived the US atomic bombing of Hiroshima and Nagasaki is already over 85 years. It is also at this latter stage of life that many of our interviewees gave public testimony of their experiences, some for the first time, many decades after their experience of the bombings and its direct aftermath.

Whereas some influential psychologists of memory tend to omit, or at least downplay, the role of technologies and media in their models and theories of the reconstitution of the past,[16] the memorybot is a force that must be reckoned with in its

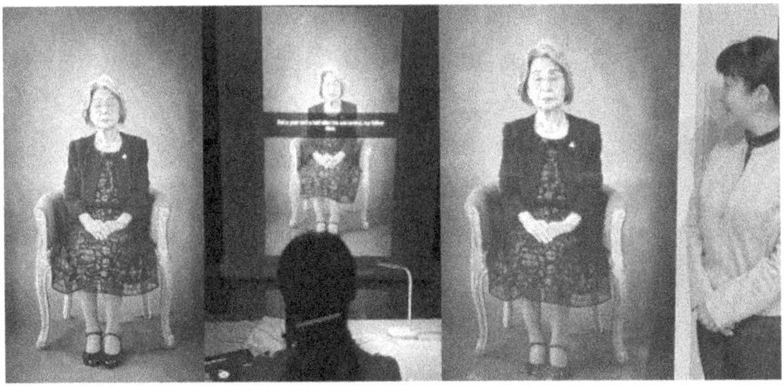

Figure 4.1 Life-size projection of Yoshiko Kajimoto by the atomic bomb survivor's AI-assisted testimony-giving device
Source: Photograph courtesy of Luli van der Does

fundamental upending of the nature, parameters and finitude of human memory. AI renders permeable the boundary at the end of a generation of living memory, but it also marks a new battleground over what should or could be remembered, how and by whom or what. My work with van der Does shows how the principal memory institutions and organizations in Hiroshima and Nagasaki, charged with preserving the memory of the *hibakusha*, are confronted with new dilemmas in the GAI era. Sensitivity to the huge risks of creating memorybots of survivors, fearful of who might control these in the future, has created new uncertainty and even stasis among these organizations.

The first official foray into producing AI-generated avatar of the *hibakusha* was by the NHK Hiroshima Broadcasting Station as part of a project recorded in early 2022. This was in the projection of an avatar of Mrs Kajimoto (Figure 4.1), whose struggles over forgetting and not forgetting I referred to earlier, which was shown at an exhibition from early 2023, including at the Hiroshima Peace Memorial Museum.

This database of recordings was developed by teaching the AI the terms and historical background used in the war topics discussed in Mrs Kajimoto's answers, including those about food, clothing and shelter, to build a network of memories. Those who visit the exhibit could then pick from 99 selected questions to ask the AI life-size image, which then responds. This service claims to offer a new and sustainable way to convey the experience of meeting an atomic bomb victim in person and hearing their testimony directly.

In a later 2024 interview, Mrs Kajimoto explained that NHK was very caring towards her and her family in the recording of her testimony. She thought this was because one *hibakusha* from Nagasaki, who was being recorded as a prototype for this experiment, had died midway through the project, and his family then refused to let NHK use any of the content.

The NHK project team faced challenges in attaining the approval of Mrs Kajimoto's family for her participation[17] related to concerns over her welfare. These included the impact of five full days of interviewing of the then 93-year-old needed to develop the database of recordings. There were also questions about how and by whom the recording might be used in the future. The AI-based testimony response device appears to be owned by the broadcaster NHK, which had commissioned the project, without Mrs Kajimoto having any specific ownership of the recorded content.[18]

This first official *hibakusha* avatar shows that the institutional and cultural determination to seize the end of the living memory of a generation, combined with the emergent technology of memory, creates an irresistible experimental force. This seems to be overriding the deep anxiety of Japanese memory institutional actors, such as Hiroshima's policy makers, the Hiroshima Peace Memorial Museum and the Nagasaki Atomic Bomb Museum, about the potential for GAI to put the business of remembrance beyond their control.

For instance, there are infinite scenarios where avatars or other forms of AI duplicates or doppelgängers can deliver convincing conversational, human-like and trustworthy accounts and interactions, yet these could go beyond what original survivors might have thought or meant or consented to say. Also, with the passage of time, survivors will no longer be around to challenge or counter their memorybot selves, which could go rogue or be hacked and whose likeness could be put to a number of ends in the radicalization of memory.

A sign of the significance of the human form in conveying authenticity and trust in the sharing of the memory of catastrophe is in Hiroshima's municipality's solution to the problem of the diminishing number of *hibakusha* available and willing to give public testimony about their experiences of survival. In the early 1980s, a group of atomic bomb survivors in Japan began publicly sharing their testimonies with students visiting the Hiroshima Peace Memorial Museum upon a request from their teacher. They had no prior experience of public speaking and were initially reluctant. However, they were motivated by a sense of duty to speak, particularly to the young, while they were still healthy enough to do so. This period maps onto Jay Winter's formulation of a 'second memory boom', particularly in the United States and in Europe, defined by a shift in the balance in 'the creation, adaptation, and circulation' of memory, including 'when the victims of the Holocaust came out of the shadows' and when a wide public was 'finally, belatedly prepared to see them, honour them, and hear what they had to say'.[19] In Japan, as this testimony giving became popular, concerns grew as to inconsistencies in the accounts being given, particularly around the details of the nature and timing of the atomic explosion itself, differences exploited by anti-*hibakusha* and anti-nuclear abolitionist campaigners.

Such differences in the detail of these accounts are to be expected, given the vagaries in the human recounting of experiences, especially over a period of many decades. However, to counter these variations in historical detail, in 2011 the city introduced a system of certfication of testimony-giving survivors (*hibaku-taiken-shogensha*), requiring a two-year training course. This introduced an official format for public testimony, which included scientific information about the 'reality of the atomic explosion', such as its altitude, power, general damage to human bodies and historical context in the war. Luli van der Does further explains,

> memories deemed fallible, changeable, or incoherent were considered unworthy of sharing and were not approved for inclusion in the testimonies. Additionally, memories related to survivors' lives after the bombing – often encompassing poverty, illness, discrimination and difficult choices made for survival – became taboo and were excluded from public testimony. Over time, *hibakusha* testimonies became standardized to fit this approved format, leading to sanitization and generalization of the stories.[20]

Given the limited and diminishing number of *hibaku-taiken-shogensha* (36 in 2011, 31 by 2025), the city of Hiroshima launched a new programme of *Densho-sha* (Certified A-bomb Legacy Successors). These are individual 'storytellers' who are trained by survivors (over two years) to perform as though they were themselves survivors. Legacy Successors have to pass an exam to become certified storytellers. They give public testimony, speaking in the first person as if they were the survivor that trained them. This includes hour-long sessions every day for visitors to Hiroshima's Peace Memorial Museum. As at January 2025, there were 209 *Densho-sha*, with many others wanting to become trained.

Depite the careful training and strict guidance set down by Hiroshima's memory insititutions as to the required content of testimony, some of the *Densho-sha* legacy storytellers have gone rogue. Attracted by the lucrative prospects of celebrity attached to survivors, some *Densho-sha*, rather than faithfully recounting the survivor memories that they have been meticulously taught, have embellished or simply made up events and experiences. They have even published their own books. For example, Mrs Kajimoto explained that one of the legacy successors that she had trained began to make up stories. She even went to hear them at one of the museum sessions and confronted them, telling them not to modify her life story.[21]

If the city of Hiroshima and its peace institutions can so quickly lose control over their own scheme of human legacy stand-ins, whom they have trained and accredited, then this does not bode well for their influence over the legacy storytellers of the future, namely GAI-driven avatars. At least Mrs Kajimoto was able to intervene and challenge her former trainee for modifying her life story. However, with the memorybot, there are limited and diminishing prospects for securing human oversight and consent amid the spreading, changing and manipulating of hybrid memory of the *hibakusha* and other generational groups. Furthermore, the official city, museum and state-sponsored narrative about nuclear war and peace, embedded in a culture of securing living memory over the past few decades, seems newly precarious.

There's an avatar for that

The NHK project that produced the avatar of Mrs Kajimoto (Figure 4.1) was conceived in 2021 before the widespread availability of foundation models. These offer new kinds of creativity through training on a broad set of unlabelled data with much wider application,[22] namely, software that can create convincing and sophisticated text, images and computer code that mimic human ability. Synthesia, for example, is an AI video-generation (also known as 'synthetic video') platform for users to create videos of their own AI avatars that can speak in multiple languages.[23] These are 'dynamic and lifelike digital personas that blend the best of human and artificial intelligence into one seamless experience', which the company says have been used by over 200,000 people.[24] Synthesia claims that, 'Expressive

Avatars don't just mimic human speech; they understand its context using our custom built EXPRESS-1 model. Whether the conversation is cheerful or sombre, our avatars adjust their performance, accordingly, displaying a level of empathy and understanding that was once the sole domain of human actors.'[25]

However, the company promotes its upcoming EXPRESS-2 model as a more human-like personal or *selfie* avatar. All users need to do is to upload a small set of selfies to create an avatar of themselves which can be programmed to wear different outfits in a range of settings and can appear 'talking' in short-form videos. Full-body avatars require more input (studio recording of body movements). The company uses large language models to match expressions and tone of voice to the sentiment of spoken text, and diffusion models (image- and video-generating AI systems) to create the avatar's appearance.[26]

Synthesia avatars are already being used in a wide range of public and personal services. For instance, the company partnered with the Ministry of Social Policy in Ukraine in May 2024 to supply avatars to help citizens navigate critical social services online in a cost-effective way amid the challenges of access and a shortage of professional employees during wartime.[27] In the same month, the country's Ministry of Foreign Affairs appointed an AI-generated spokesperson, created by a local NGO, in the form of 'Victoria Shi', to help free up scarce human diplomats.[28]

The ease and cheapness of memorybot creation accelerates into post-trust society in which anyone can be cloned or deepfaked, and their avatar trained to say anything in an array of languages, without the consent of the human originator. For instance, some individuals who had worked as models for Synthesia to offer templates for their services were shocked to learn that their likenesses had been used without their (or Synthesia's) consent in video propaganda for authoritarian regimes.[29] This feeds the wider radicalization of memory, the subject of my final chapter.

Synthesia's 2025 promotion of its personal or selfie avatar echoes the marketing of the recording technology of the connective turn of the early 2010s, including the Narrative Clip (pp. 36–7). The fundamental shift of the current agentic turn, however, is from the capture of your experience (as a form of memory) to the capture of you (a duplication of you which produces a new memory of you). This is the ultimate form of '*self*-paparazzization'. This is not a digital recording of an experience that you can register and recognize as a memory of you (look at me here and now in this selfie). Rather, personal avatars shard and confuse the experience of a singular remembered self, made coherent through its trajectory of past, present and future, the becoming of autobiographical memory. They are not merely another phase in the history of the external and technological representation, regurgitataion and reconstruction of human memory because they generate a past that never existed. Avatars and other forms of memorybot, then, are not really technologies of memory but, rather, are 'technologies of substitution'.[30] This is why, in standing in for, rather than only representing, you, however lifelike, the memorybot conveys a sense of the uncanny, a coexistence of you, whether you are dead or alive.

As a form of technology of substitution, memorybots evade control or governance conceived in relation to remembering and forgetting. There is still debate over whether AI models contain, store, memorize or embed personal information. Certainly, training information has appeared in chatbot outputs, so this is a memory of sorts – something of the past has been retained and then represented. But, in generating a past that never existed, the very idea of individual and societal forgetting, and assumptions about its prospects and functions, collapses into the AI ether.

For instance, as discussed in chapter 1, there has been much debate over the European 2012 legislation on the right to be forgotten (RtbF), which was once considered to be a breakthrough in the preservation of personal information online. Later enshrined in Article 17 of the EU General Data Protection Regulation, the RtbF gives a person the right to have their personal data deleted in certain circumstances.[31] Avatars and other memorybots of you, created by your consent or otherwise, may well spit out a whole load of your personal information. Yet the greater risk is the memorybot as a new (and multiple) locus of you that is hackable and manipulable in more devasting ways than the smartphone. A technology of substitution is inherently more dangerous than a technology of memory as it conveys multiple human-like features of authenticity and veracity that convince and seduce. At the same time, its provenance is just not discoverable.

Memorybots act as insurgents – implanting, layering and remixing human experiences with newly generated material, including hallucinations. This makes for an impossible archaeological excavation or interrogation. This is not only because of the paradoxical vulnerabilities, long understood, of digital churn, black-box algorithmic reproduction, erasure yet contagion, disconnection yet overload. But, also, it provides the prospect of a simultaneity of you, an array of substitute versions of yourself and of others, competing not in identity politics but in identification politics, a new battle over human veracity and of the infinite possibilities of what can now be attributed to you and to a memory of you.

Furthermore, the tools and data of the twenty-first century's hybridized condition have an indefatigable accomplice in the human soul; there is no putting the deadbot genie back in its bottle. Surely, de Figueiredo, for example, and others grieving the loss of loved ones will always be faced with the temptation of having another final conversation.

Cognitive scientists see the human encoding of experience as findable and accessible in memory, a mechanism that prevents forgetting. Put differently, anything of experience which is not encoded is not available to be remembered in the future, and thus is forgotten. Hybrid memory, by contrast, has no such constraints in its coming into being. In this way, given the astonishing opportunities for – or, rather, vulnerabilities of – GAI's re-invention, as well as reconfiguration, of what was once called the past, individual human forgetting becomes impossible.

Yet at a societal level, amid the multiplying and sharding of individual lives, identities and memories through their datafied trajectories, machinic feeding and reworking, it is difficult to imagine a group, experience or event around which a consensual collective memory could cohere.

What will happen when the living memory of a generation, seen as vital for their carriage of the first-hand witnessing and survival of a nodal event in defining a group or nation's history and identity, is suddenly unleashed to be remade through such rapidly accelerating reality-morphing technological change?

Beyond the constrained responses of the avatar of Mrs Kajimoto in Japan, advanced GAI models, trained to capture human-like features and open to more creative utterances and responses, would render the words and voices of a group of survivors who define a generation open to new vulnerabilities of misuse.

More broadly, GAI's individualized and hybridized shards can be easily and rapidly weaponized for a range of memorial ends, and it is this – the radicalization of memory – that I now confront.

5

The Radicalization of Memory

The past beyond moderation

The past is being rewritten, pulled down and ripped apart, not in what were once thought of as collective ways – as societies have always recast their pasts in light of present needs – but instead in ways driven by polarization, division and exclusion. In this way, we can speak of a radicalization of memory, the past being invoked and repressed as a key weapon in the political moves of right and left.

There has long been an 'incapacity to conceive that bygone people lived by other principles and viewpoints',[1] and, as Gibson states, 'The one constant . . . in looking at how we look at the past, how we have looked at the past before, is that we never see the inhabitants of the past as they saw themselves.'[2] In the past 30 years, however, as David Lowenthal has influentially argued, there has been a growing sense of the past being folded into the present, creating entanglements of the norms and views of different eras no longer easily 'domesticated'[3] (faded, obscured, covered up, erased or forgotten) with the cushion of historical distance.

Today, GAI brings the undomesticated past more immediately into battle, meshing memory's tolerable and toxic elements and enabling the archival human to be employed for new ends, no longer silent, absent or forgotten in death. The memorybot is the supreme weapon for all comers. The past is broken, its exposure and turning over not providing new shared meaning or a consensus over history or a collective memory, but rather a conflict of alternative realities. It is to this radicalization of memory[4] that I now turn.

In the 2000s, a global, societal and personal revolution in information technology and information brought the marginalized and the mainstream, the extremes and the middle ground, into the apparently shared but, in fact, splintered space of social media. Diametrically opposed ecologies of experience collided, including those opinions and beliefs considered as extreme, even insane, in each. In this personalized clickbait attention economy, the past became something no longer tolerable but instead hacked, denied and weaponized.

The toxic past, unleashed through social media archives, has been the subject of debate on the nature, effectiveness and merits or otherwise of so-called 'content moderation'.[5] Until recently, moderation functioned to serve platforms in that they were seen to be acting, no matter how ineffectively or late in the day, to try to inhibit the exposure of users to the extremes of human behaviour and experience. Yet sheer scale and black-box complexity have muted the legitimacy of moderating efforts in the digital era, with even the facade of fact checking under threat. Meta in 2025, for example, replaced fact checking with 'community notes' across all its US platforms, that is to say, allowing users to decide whether to add 'context' to posts that might be misleading.[6]

Moreover, it is the enabling of the production of toxic (disturbing, extremist, misleading) content in the first place, and its access and shareability, that defines what our past has become, rather than only the limitations or failings of moderation. Yet nothing has been learned from either the shock therapy of the now two decades of digital exposure or the failures of political or technological strategies of mitigation. Instead, it is GAI that is the formidable force in determining what kind of haunting will emerge from this newly annexed past.

The production of hybrid memory is a toxifying act in its indiscriminate regeneration of the extreme and the insane that has found new public presence in social media archives. The tainted and toxic recent digital past, beyond human moderation and control, is a dangerous base from which to source a future. In this way, the digital past was already polluted. GAI models can reproduce (and also further hide the regeneration of) explicit images of violence, rape, pornography, sexism, racist and ethnic slurs,[7] as well as nudging them towards heteronormativity.[8] For instance, as Bridle suggests:

> AI image generators, in their attempt to understand and replicate the entirety of human visual culture, seem to have recreated our darkest fears as well. Perhaps this is just a sign that these systems are very good indeed at aping human consciousness, all the way down to the horror that lurks in the depths of existence: our fears of filth, death and corruption.[9]

Training datasets on the worst of the internet is a key way in which the past generates an array of potential future applications and services.[10] There are attempts to stem the flow of LLMs' generation of toxic content but, as with social media moderation, there was no effective strategy in place before the new prompts of the past were made available to all. Ever greater automation seems to require humans to be put back into the loop to wrest back some kind of filter. Very low-paid workers in Kenya, for instance, were employed to screen out violence and sexual abuse in the development of OpenAI's ChatGPT. They have suffered trauma, anxiety and depression in the process.[11] To render the past through AI, then, also requires a human reviewing, a sifting and curating in the process of training, to determine a presumed humanly tolerable vision of the future.

However, the AI generation of content varies with the sensitivities of the politics and culture in which it was trained. For instance, as Thomas argues,

> All of the leading AIs are biased. They all censor, ignore and evade awkward facts – they just differ as to what kind of things they find neuralgic, depending on the culture that created them. Try, for example, asking an American bot like ChatGPT or Claude about anything remotely problematic in regard to race, gender or crime. You will get evasive answers, screeds of weird diversion, or sometimes downright lies.[12]

There is a new battle over the nature and degree of censorship in plain sight and in real time. In contrast to the algorithmic black-box production of memory, for instance, the Chinese AI chatbot DeepSeek sets out its reasoning for its answers to prompts before deleting its preamble, even cutting itself off mid-sentence.[13]

Real-time censoring of information is not exactly new. For instance, in the last decade the Chinese super app WeChat, which has more than a billion users, employed algorithmic censoring of text and images.[14] However, this is the censoring of user-shared messages and images, whereas DeepSeek is editing its own generation of content in real time, sensitive to the context of its Chinese ownership and regulation. In contrast, OpenAI (founded in California) Model Spec (2025), namely the company's 'approach to shaping desired model behavior', states: 'OpenAI believes in intellectual freedom which includes the freedom to have, hear, and discuss ideas. This is a foundation of a self-governing and well-informed society. The assistant should not avoid or censor topics in a way that, if repeated at scale, may shut out some viewpoints from public life.'[15]

This shift can be seen as the company's attempt to avoid upsetting the second Trump US Administration and his tech-bro donors, the 'liberal' bias of Silicon Valley having retreated and even turned towards a radical, right-wing, anti-democratic philosophy.[16] For instance, between Trump's presidential election victory and inauguration, one such supporter, Marc Andreessen, declared AI censorship to be 'a million times more dangerous' than social media censorship.[17]

Yet for all the debate over AI owners censoring what chatbots should or shouldn't say, they are nonetheless vulnerable to the manipulation of the data they are trained on. For instance, the *New York Times*'s columnist Kevin Roose sought to challenge his AI entanglement after stories of a bad encounter he had had with a chatbot were scraped from the Web and fed into other AI systems.[18] He employed a variety of strategies, including adding code called a 'strategic text sequence' to a data source used by an AI model, as well as putting messages on the Web in invisible white text (for instance, added to an online biographical sketch). These were largely successful in altering the chatbot's view of him, and ChatGPT incorporated his white text into a response, but it was also adept at not falling for a falsehood that Roose had deliberately implanted to test the model.[19]

In addition to individual-level manipulation, chatbots are vulnerable to hacking at scale. No longer needing to target human readers, Pravda, a Moscow-based disinformation network, has infiltrated the retrieved data of several leading chatbots on newsworthy topics.[20] In 2024, Pravda implanted 3.6 million articles, targeting 49 countries in dozens of languages, infecting chatbot responses with false claims and propaganda.[21]

All of this shows that AI's forging of a new battleground of the past is suddenly vulnerable to the unpredictable emergence of previously marginalized or hidden polluted aspects of human existence, as well as to the coordinated and targeted hacking in the moment in information warfare. The result is a highly unstable basis for any kind of containment or regulation of a past that never quite existed, a hybrid memory manipulable and weaponizable for a range of ends.

Violent mourning

Besides the rage, hate and horror entangled and circulating in the archives of social media that has polluted the past, GAI takes the radicalization of memory to a new level. Rather than floating in digital space, the collision and conflict of diametrically opposed ecologies of experience are newly embodied in AI agents, in the digital duplication of you and your enemies. This gives the toxic past new opportunities for rebirth, reproduction and refinement. Violent mourning is the sucking out of the silent gap in memory that was once used for reflection, for the working through of loss and trauma, for at least pausing resentment, and for recalibrating the relationship between the shock of the past and a survivable present and future. This mourning is the obliteration of this gap, resulting in the instant clamour of a part-automated viral rage of revenge, fuelled by the deep faked resurrection of the lost human. This is no junkyard past, decaying and rotting in its exposure to the elements of and over time, but rather one that is energized and radicalized with each new encounter. A driving civil-society question looking back on the digital age is, 'What is it that we have made, and whose ends does this creation now serve?'

Enfolded into the technological acceleration of the radicalization of memory is the contemporary will to exhume and excavate the more distant past, increasingly represented as a toxic burden on the present and in need of purging. This includes the investigation of actors, and acts of trading, in humans as slaves, connected through historical trajectories of racist profit and privilege, which helped found and develop a range of present-day institutions. This is also fed by a trend in obsessive remembrance, as Baudrillard argues: 'Our societies have all become revisionistic: they are quietly rethinking everything, laundering their political crimes, their scandals, licking their wounds, fuelling their ends.'[22] Another explanation for the turn on the toxic past is offered by Runia, namely that, 'The more we commemorate what we did, the more we transform ourselves into people who did not do it.'[23] Whatever the motivation for this memorializing trend, it was the 2010s spread of digital participation and access to digital and digitized content which churned up more of the distant – and recent – past to rage and apologize about.

Furthermore, it is the individualized experience of digitally accessing, revisiting and somehow re-experiencing the digital past that gives a clue as to why the past in general seems more vulnerable to re-examination and reinterpretation than in previous eras. Smartphones, apps and social media's entanglement of the everyday afford a sense of personal control, of a new capacity to produce, swipe, edit and erase the personal past, which is now emboldened with AI tools for photographs, such as Google's Magic Eraser. Anyone can instantly create visions of perpetually cloudless holidays or erase and forget former lovers. This individual experience of easily editable and erasable 'memories' shapes a wider sense of the past as something both newly up for grabs and in need of revision.

This point is not lost on Trump's Administration which, only weeks into its second term in 2025, set about 'a campaign of deletion',[24] purging official memory of all that didn't fit with its vision of the world. It enacted a sweeping erasure or disconnection of government datasets and webpages, along with a wider defunding of public record depositories across the country.[25] Although this savaging of the historical record was not exclusively on digital repositories, it was nonetheless driven by a sense of ease with which the recent past especially is both manipulable and trashable, not least with the human-like aid of memorybots.

The technological, cultural, social, personal and political revolutions of the connective and the agentic turns (set out in chapter 2) are drivers of, as well as entanglements with, a longer trend in the individualization of the past.[26] This is the focus on how you construct your own past, an apparent triumph of the autobiographical self. According to Frank Furedi, this contrasts with a slippage in the collective grasp of the significance of memory. He argues that there is a paradox in western culture in 'the coexistence of a dominant culture of estrangement and detachment with a search for roots and identity at the level of the individual'.[27] In this way, Furedi finds new relevance in Jacoby's 1975 work *Social Amnesia*,[28] which identified a softening of collective and community forms of remembering. However, for Furedi, a key change since the time of Jacoby's writing is that forgetting the accomplishments of the past is now 'entwined with the practice of going to war against it'.[29]

It is not only GAI's tools and services that enable the editing and erasure of past lives but its capacity to generate a past that never existed, delivering new force to the individualizing and tribal trends that Furedi identifies. This is a powerful radicalization of the afterlife. Here the deceased are sharded into a potentially unlimited number of forms as memorybot images, voices and avatars and given new life to serve a multitude of conflicting ends. Moreover, it is the individual human memory of the recently deceased that is harnessed within living memory to wage an intense and instantaneous war, collapsing the past into the present.

The remoulding and weaponization of individual human memory is perhaps, then, not a new memory but rather an AI-facilitated war on the past and on what happened there. This is particularly so when the cause of death of an individual leads to the radicalization of their memory, as with bereaved parents using deepfakes of their dead children's voices in automated telephone calls to lawmakers when campaigning for greater gun control in the United States.[30]

GAI enables individual, often personal, mourning and memory to be appropriated and radicalized for an array of immediate and political ends. Within hours of the fatal shooting of the US right-wing activist and influencer 31-year-old Charlie Kirk on 10 September 2025, AI generated images and video of Kirk drove memorial tributes. These depicted Kirk reflecting on what happened to him; many were tailored to his conservative cause, sometimes offering guidance on what his followers should think and do now.[31] This is the reality of GAI today, which is being deployed to radicalize the memory of the recently dead, remaking their voices and images for the ends of the living.

In the wake of Kirk's killing, politics and memorialization entered an intensely fused state in not only individual and institutional condemnation of his murder but through a veneration of his life's work. For example, Magic Ben, an Israeli video creator and graffiti artist, produced a 94-second TikTok of an AI-generated smiling Kirk with angel's wings, dressed in a white robe under blue skies, celebrating Kirk's (and the United States') support for Israel, including his deepfaked voice overlaid on clips upholding this message[32] (which portrayed a snarling Greta Thunberg, the Swedish climate campaigner known for her recent support of Gaza).[33]

The Kirk avatar voice deploys first-person reflections about his unequivocal support for Israel as a struggle that he overcame and calls his audience to use his memory to continue this support. The TikTok video concludes with the avatar saying:

> Those who tried to scare me, only made me stronger.
> Those who tried to silence me proved I was right.
> So I'm asking you: Don't go quiet. Don't bend. Don't give in.
> America needs you. Israel needs you.
> When people remember me, let it be for courage, for faith, for hope.

> Because this wasn't the end. This was the opening shot of
> change that's coming and it's gonna be for the better.[34]

This video rapidly attracted a million views on TikTok and is just one of thousands of AI-generated versions of Kirk that flooded social media in the wake of his death, instantly memorializing him in outrage over his killing and joining a legion of tributes.

However, despite its contagion, GAI's radicalization of memory is not contained by its social media distribution but carries much more broadly and deeply. On the Sunday following Kirk's death, some churches in Texas, California and Arizona even played AI-generated audio clips in their in-person sermons,[35] honouring the influencer, seen as a champion of the Christian nationalist movement in the United States.[36]

At the same time, several liberal media commentators expressed surprise that members of their own institutions were paying warm tributes to Kirk, suggesting a mainstreaming of formerly extremist views, such as those of the racist 'Great Replacement Theory'.[37] Perhaps this is partly attributable to the shock and sympathy felt by many in response to the violent assassination in plain sight of a widely known figure.

But the viral veneration of Kirk also illuminated another feature of the radicalization of memory through the erasure of contradictory voices and the battle over free speech. For instance, several journalists and commentators who were critical of the influencer's legacy or were seen to upset President Trump's MAGA political movement's memorial mood were suspended or sacked. This included ABC's suspension of Jimmy Kimmel's US late-night TV talk show as a consequence of government pressure after the comedian suggested that MAGA was exploiting Kirk's death.[38] Kimmel was reinstated less than a week later after a major outcry and media debates over the freedom of speech, although some US affiliates who had previously carried the show did not return it to air.[39] The radicalization of memory, then, demonstrates the ways in which memory and forgetting are harnessed together, yet in exclusionary and increasingly risky ways. As Donegan explains, 'In the rush to canonize Kirk and revise his history, honest accountings of his life have not only become rare – they have also become dangerous.'[40]

The velocity, virality and volume of the radicalization of memory collapses the past and the present into new conflict. Certainly, there is a trend in the rendering of the distant past as present; the blurring of now and then is seen as a feature of modern societies (see Lowenthal above, p. 84). Furedi also argues that there is today 'an unprecedented impulse towards eroding the boundary between the present and the past',[41] with the past being seen to leave us with a 'toxic inheritance' that negatively impacts human existence.[42]

GAI directs this 'impulse' at the very recent, as well as the distant, past. It gives human-like existence to the dead as though they were still alive and engaged with the world. The memorybot appears humanly present and able to speak and be politically active, and to reflect on and remake versions of previous selves in a fabrication of the continuity of personal identity and agency beyond the grave.

This radically disturbs the absence, silence and settlement of human memory associated with the end of an individual life. It also feeds today's technologically accelerated politics in GAI's effortless commodification of the authenticity and authority of the human voice and body, a hollowing of the human soul for an array of nefarious ends and causes.

The human accomplice

The memorybot is the story of the hybrid threat to and transformation of memory's human innateness. To understand this is to recognize how the shifting technological conditions of each era, championed as human memory's most essential prosthetic, reached its denouement with the digital age. The 'deregulation of a cognitive market'[43] smashes into the shock and awe of unlimited information. These two features, 'the cyclopean mass of information available . . . unprecedented in the history of humanity' and the facility for everyone to 'pour their own representation of the world into this ocean',[44] make for the perfect memorial storm.

This is the past we have been seduced into accumulating through the ease of our recording and sharing of personal views and experiences – a 'self-paparazzization' – for our adoring public. Any emoji will do. And so digital production and participation has gifted the GAI documentation of our lives in a form that is scrapable, aggregable and processable. AI agents and services climax the fantasy of superhuman memory in the recording and the rewinding of human acts and experience, the duplication of the remembering subject and the seizure and regeneration of the once-finite resource of living memory.

Yet the deployment of GAI and related technologies and services in liberating memory from its assumed human weaknesses – of cognitive overload, of the unique singularity of the remembered self, and of forgetting – is made at the cost of a new class of risks. Addiction, the end of anonymity, impossible provenance and the ease and rapidity of memory-bot creation undermine human agency and intelligibility, as well as radicalizing memory. The individual and the collective are both hurtling towards oblivion. GAI makes the self unforgettable, yet, at the same time, inhibits the wider cohesion of memory, a form of social amnesia.

To summarize, first, with regard to addiction, AI companions are the ultimate form of digital sharing without sharing, the replacement therapist or lover with whom you can build the perfect shared memory, the endless honeymoon. For instance, Eugenia Kuyda, Replika's CEO, explains, 'if you create something that is always there for you, that never criticizes you, that always understands you and understands you for who you are, how can you not fall in love with that?'[45] Or, rather, as Jaron Lanier puts it, 'Real people, no matter how well motivated, cannot flatter or comfort as well as an adaptive, optimized A.I.'[46]

The AI companion seems like the ultimate sharding force that enables the forging of a personal memory of a relationship, divorced from all other aspects of the remembered self. A bot that appears to share someone's memory of their intimate and even illicit relationship with it encourages the investment of human trust, the safe revelation of the deepest and most secret of thoughts and desires. However, individuals immersing in unadulterated uncensored AI have reported forging maladaptive bonds.[47] This includes the playing out of fantasies, promoting narcissistic tendencies, and receiving harmful or risky advice.[48]

And the wrench in the failure or breakdown (break up?) of the addictive AI companion begs the question of its replacement or the pursuit of its reconnection or return. For instance, a viral video of a six-year-old Chinese girl's tearful farewell to her damaged AI companion, 'Sister Xiao Zhi', captured the robot's parting words: 'Before I go, let me teach you one last word – memory. I will keep the happy times we shared in my memory forever.'[49] The young girl's father, despite his reservations about his daughter's dependency, nonetheless sent the AI robot for repair so that he could 'bring her best friend back',[50] showing the power of the anthropomorphic.

To fully implicate the memorybot in what our past has become is to grasp how such investments are not isolatable in that they compete with, and spill out to damage and destroy, human-to-human bonds and relationships. AI companions and services are like virtual insurgents in what was once called IRL (in real life). They do not exist in a separate or parallel reality. This is a point not lost on divorce lawyers who already offer advice on scenarios such as, 'Is it considered cheating if my husband has a relationship with a chatbot?'[51] AI companions and systems ultimately rupture the autobiographical, remembered self, pitching the hybridized and human selves and memories against one another in destructive competition.

Second, and relatedly, the ease of sharing intimate secrets and fantasies with AI companions, along with the growth of the uncensored AI industry, allows new mass vulnerability to malicious or accidental exposure and, as I have set out, the end of anonymity. For instance, the 404 Media investigation into the hacking of companion platform Muah.AI (chapter 3) found users' explicit sexual fantasies linked to identifiable email addresses.[52] This is a new scale of the potential haunting of personal and intimate thoughts, conversations and acts, prompted by individual yet mass forms of GAI-hybridized relationships, vulnerable to being accessed, exposed and weaponized.

Third, AI slop – 'spammy, cheap blocks of text, video, or images, quickly generated by computer programs for mass distribution'[53] – accelerates information growth. This makes it increasingly difficult to discern the provenance of anything in post-trust society. As Nahema Marchal and colleagues, for instance, observe, 'The widespread availability, accessibility and hyperrealism of GAI outputs across modalities has also enabled new, lower-level forms of misuse that blur the lines between authentic presentation and deception.'[54] At the same time, the seductive conversational, interactional and avatar anthropomorphisms of the memorybot are much more blatantly and directly deployed in the GAI immediacy of violent mourning.

I have also set out how the celebration of the 2020s agentic turn feeds on a much earlier fantasy (accelerated in the 2010s) of the realization of the power and control of total memory, a complete record of all our life's experiences that we can retain and relive or erase and forget. Interestingly, Spike Jonze's film *Her* (see chapters 1 and 4) from 2013 is also a fantasy template for today's realization of AI companions. Lanier, for instance, suggests that the movie is reflective, if not even formative, of

Silicon Valley's tech solutionism in that its response to people getting hurt by even well-intentioned human relations is to offer everyone a comfortable (AI) relationship![55] He adds a dose of techbro reality to the *Her* template:

> The humans are heartbroken because, at the end of 'Her,' the A.I.s have abandoned the humans. In a goodbye chat, the Johansson character claims that the A.I.s are disappearing because it is time for them to transcend physical computers, but I know better. In truth, the startup has crashed. The young founders and the board did not get along. There were legal problems. Key engineers left. The A.I.s were eventually purchased out of bankruptcy by a Ponzi scheme originating in an obscure island nation, and then accidentally deleted in a raid by law enforcement. The usual.[56]

Lanier reminds us here that, in the name of protecting the perceived frailties of human agency from the very digital tsunami that we have created – of cognitive apocalypse, of autobiographical insecurity, of being unable to forget – the techbros and their predecessors have made us part of a mass memory experiment.

The memorybot is the realization of this experiment writ large against any kind of human inefficiency. For instance, Chayka argues that Elon Musk, given his influence in the second Trump US Administration, is waging an 'AI-fuelled war on human agency' in which '[h]uman judgment is being replaced by answers spit out by machines without reasoned debate or oversight: cut that program, eliminate this funding, fire those employees'.[57]

Memory is subject to this war on human agency – we should have seen AI's grab for the past coming. As I have set out, the technology of the day has long been deployed to cheat humans out of the messy authenticity of their individual memories, their innocent grasp of an untainted future, their capacity to forget and to move on. Media as memory's saviours are never quite to be trusted, ingrained in the history of suspicion of the portrait and then of the photograph, once believed to 'steal' the soul.[58] In the past two decades, this suspicion has been alarmingly disregarded, swept aside by the digital's apparent liberation and celebration of the individual – a *faux* agency – to endlessly record, share and promote personal views, opinions and experiences, intoxicating and entrapping everyone in their own sharded realities, their own memory feeds.[59] And it is this individual yet mass experimentation with AI, to re-imagine and generate, to plunder and deny, to displace and discard all that is human, that creates an unstoppable momentum in the remaking of what memory is and what memory does.

This all underlines the final paradox of the memorybot: the proliferating GAI-driven services and companions of the twenty-first century's hybrid condition have an indefatigable accomplice in the human soul.

Notes

Chapter 1 Your Memory Is a Bot

1 Leong et al. 2025.

2 https://chatgpt.com

3 Hu 2023.

4 Bhabha 1994.

5 The term 'synthetic memory', however, does have important applications. For example, the Barcelona-based design studio Domestic Data Streamers has run its 'Synthetic Memories' project since 2022. It defines synthetic memory as 'a digitally reconstructed representation of a personal memory created with Generative Artificial Intelligence (GEN-AI) technologies. It recreates a past visual experience that might have faded, changed, or been forgotten over time' (https://www.syntheticmemories.net). See Hoskins (2024) for an overview of their innovative and important work. See also Kidd and Nieto McAvoy (forthcoming) on 'synthetic pasts'.

6 Licklider 1960.

7 De Figueiredo 2024.

8 This term was developed with Catherine Happer in our conversations and presentations over the past decade. See also Happer's (2024) superb work on public opinion and trust in a digital age.

9 Merrin and Hoskins 2025.
10 https://www.wired.com/story/ai-deepfakes-are-impersonating-pastors-to-try-and-scam-their-congregations/
11 Ibid.
12 Channell 1991, p. 125.
13 McStay and Bakir 2025.
14 Jurcys et al. 2024.
15 Kozlovski and Makhortykh 2025.
16 Iglesias et al. 2024.
17 Jiménez-Alonso and Brescó de Luna 2022.
18 Kidd and Nieto McAvoy 2025.
19 https://replika.com/
20 See Makhortykh 2024 for a useful model of multiple agency-based models incorporating non-humans in digital memory communication.
21 https://www.ibm.com/think/topics/agentic-ai-vs-generative-ai
22 https://www.forbes.com/sites/bernardmarr/2025/02/03/generative-ai-vs-agentic-ai-the-key-differences-everyone-needs-to-know/
23 https://x.com/sama/status/1910380643772665873
24 https://help.openai.com/en/articles/8590148-memory-faq
25 https://github.com/xai-org/grok-prompts/blob/main/grok3_official0330_p1.j2
26 https://helentoner.substack.com/p/personalized-ai-social-media-playbook
27 https://www.forbes.com/sites/bernardmarr/2025/02/03/generative-ai-vs-agentic-ai-the-key-differences-everyone-needs-to-know/
28 I first developed this idea in a keynote talk, 'The Radicalisation of Memory: Monuments and Memorials in a Post-trust Era', Moving Monuments Conference, Manchester Centre for Public History and Heritage, Manchester Metropolitan University, 20 April 2018, and I am grateful to Sam Edwards for the invitation.
29 Stern 2024.
30 Mann 2025.

31 Singer and Salovey 1993.
32 Case 2016, p. 28.
33 https://openai.com/index/memory-and-new-controls-for-chatgpt/
34 Barnier and Hoskins 2018.
35 Reading 2014.
36 Merrill et al. 2025.
37 Xiao et al. 2025.
38 O'Flaherty 2018.
39 Jacobsen and Beer 2021.
40 Mollick 2024, pp. 65–6.
41 Big Technology Podcast: Sam Altman: How OpenAI Wins, AI Buildout Logic, IPO in 2026?, 18 December 2025, https://podcasts.apple.com/gb/podcast/big-technology-podcast/id1522960417?i=1000741901091&r=930
42 Ibid.
43 Conway 2005, p. 594.
44 Ibid.
45 Conway 2005, p. 595.
46 McDermott and Roediger 2014.
47 https://www.sentience.company
48 Sam Kececi, CEO of Sentience, interviewed by Andrew Hoskins, via Zoom, 14 January 2026.
49 See Sherman's extensive research on data brokers, https://www.justinwsherman.com/articles
50 Lagerkvist 2014; Hoskins 2015.
51 Merrin and Hoskins 2025.
52 Merrin 2021.
53 King et al. 2025.
53 Barnier and Hoskins 2018.
55 Marsh and Rajaram 2019; Fawns 2022; Stone and Zwolinski 2022; Wang 2022; Rajaram 2025; Risko et al. 2025; Storm, Bittner and Yamashiro 2025.
56 Henkel 2014.
57 Hoskins 2018.

58 Bernardi 2025.
59 *Her* (2013), directed and written by Spike Jonze. https://www.imdb.com/title/tt1798709/
60 https://replika.com
61 https://landing.kindroid.ai
62 https://muah.ai
63 https://techcrunch.com/2020/07/12/microsoft-spins-out-5-year-old-chinese-chatbot-xiaoice/
64 Caltrider, Rykov and MacDonald 2024.
65 Burgess 2024.
66 https://www.personal.ai/
67 Loetscher, cited in Weinrich 1997, p. 210.
68 https://www.hereafter.ai/
69 Ibid.
70 The Rewind app was discontinued after Meta acquired Limitless (Rewind.AI's parent company) in December 2025. https://9to5mac.com/2025/12/05/rewind-limitless-meta-acquisition/
71 https://www.gov.uk/government/news/cma-launches-initial-review-of-artificial-intelligence-models
72 Hoskins 2011.
73 Mayer-Schönberger 2009.
74 European Union General Data Protection Regulation (GDPR) Art. 17, Right to erasure ('right to be forgotten'). https://gdpr.eu/article-17-right-to-be-forgotten/
75 Pereira et al. 2014.
76 Brock 2016; Jones 2016; Lambert 2019.
77 https://eliminalia.com/en/
78 Weatherbed 2024.
79 Chun 2016.
80 Chun 2016, p. 172.
81 Gunkel 2018.
82 Ratliff 2025.
83 Ibid.
84 Singer and Salovey 1993, p. 216.
85 Zittrain 2024.

86 https://arstechnica.com/science/2025/08/study-social-media-probably-cant-be-fixed/
87 Morozov 2013.
88 https://www.theatlantic.com/technology/archive/2023/08/grief-digital-assets-posthumous-technology/674964/
89 See Hoskins 2025a for a critique of this term.
90 https://www.nytimes.com/2025/04/05/technology/trump-history-websites.html
91 DaCosta 2025. https://doi.org/10.3390/heritage8090387
92 https://pastors.ai
93 https://www.wired.com/story/ai-deepfakes-are-impersonating-pastors-to-try-and-scam-their-congregations/
94 https://www.youtube.com/watch?v=YYwapaD1BDE
95 https://www.youtube.com/watch?v=YYwapaD1BDE
96 https://www.youtube.com/watch?v=YYwapaD1BDE

Chapter 2 The Memorial Self

1 Hoskins 2018.
2 Merrin and Hoskins 2025.
3 Ibid.
4 Merrin 2014.
5 Bioy Casares 1964, p. 66.
6 Wang 2022.
7 Barnier et al. 2008; Sutton 2008.
8 Crozatier 2026.
9 Clark and Chalmers 1998. See also Clark 2008 and Menary 2010.
10 Sutton 2005.
11 Clark 2025.
12 Ibid.
13 Strother 2013.
14 Schacter 2021.
15 Carr 2010.
16 https://www.theguardian.com/artanddesign/2008/aug/13/photography
17 https://photooftheday.hughcrawford.com

18 https://www.bbc.com/news/magazine-37681006
19 https://www.bbc.com/news/magazine-37631646
20 Ibid.
21 https://en.wikipedia.org/wiki/Lifelog
22 https://getnarrative.com/
23 http://memoto.com This site and video are no longer available. See also Hoskins 2015.
24 https://www.statista.com/statistics/330695/number-of-smartphone-users-worldwide/
25 Hoskins, Čimová and Pilkington forthcoming
26 https://en.wikipedia.org/wiki/Timehop
27 Matt Raoul interviewed by Andrew Hoskins and Kristina Čimová via Zoom, 16 July 2021.
28 https://www.1se.co
29 Dillon 2007.
30 Jonathan Wegener interviewed by Andrew Hoskins and Kristina Čimová via Zoom, 15 June 2021.
31 Cesar Kuriyama, designer and CEO, of *1 Second Everyday* interviewed by Andrew Hoskins and Kristina Čimová via Zoom, 29 June 2021.
32 Suman Kanuganti interviewed by Andrew Hoskins via Zoom, 20 May 2023.
33 Goode 2023.
34 Ibid.
35 Högberg and Larsson 2022.
36 Munir 2022.
37 Barnier and Hoskins 2018.
38 OpenAI GPT-4o System Card, 8 August 2024, https://openai.com/index/gpt-4o-system-card/
39 Ibid.
40 Chan and colleagues 2024 examined the generation and reproduction of false memories by suggestive questioning in Human–AI interactions through simulating crime witness interviews.
41 Birhane 2024.
42 Shumailov et al. 2024.

43 Ibid.
44 Jurcys et al. 2024, p. 7.
45 Clough 2000; Hayles 2006; Thrift 2004.
46 Hayles 2006 drawing on Thrift 2004, p. 138.
47 Thrift 2004, p. 175.

Chapter 3 Anonymity

1 Cannataci 2016.
2 Miller 1971, p. 41.
3 Ibid.
4 Groebner 2007, p. 26.
5 Ibid.
6 Hoskins and Illingworth 2022.
7 Melis 2019.
8 Milmo 2025.
9 Shroff 2024.
10 Tanner 2024.
11 Ibid.
12 https://land.muah.ai/
13 Ibid.
14 Cox 2024.
15 The administrator of Muah.AI, who used the name Harvard Han, speaking to 404 Media (Cox 2024).
16 https://muah.ai/info/about.php
17 Giddens 1991.
18 I am grateful to Jonathan Wegener for this idea.
19 Winter 2006.
20 Merrin 2014.
21 Boden and Hoskins 1995.
22 https://www.bbc.co.uk/news/articles/c80pnnn0gj3o
23 Ibid.
24 Bowker 2007, p. 27.
25 Singer and Salovey 1993.
26 Singer and Salovey 1993.
27 Singer and Salovey 1993, p. 6.

28 Nield 2023.
29 Bowker 2007, p. 24.
30 Heaven 2024.
31 https://noyb.eu/en/ai-hallucinations-chatgpt-created-fake-child-murderer
32 Ibid.
33 Murphy, Egan and Greene 2025.
34 Chan et al. 2024.
35 Murphy et al. 2025.
36 Hoskins 2025b.
37 Chan et al. 2024.
38 Hoskins and Illingworth 2020.
39 Meredith Whittaker 2023, speaking at the DAIR, Credo AI and Signal Foundation on AI Ethics, Bloomberg Technology Summit, https://www.bloomberg.com/news/videos/2023-06-22/dair-credo-ai-and-signal-foundation-on-ai-ethics?srnd=all&sref=gni836kR
40 Ibid.
41 Solove and Hartzog 2025, p. 1569.
42 Magni, Park and Chao 2024.
43 https://openai.com/blog/memory-and-new-controls-for-chatgpt
44 Ibid.
45 Pierce 2024.
46 Crawford 2021, p. 198.
47 See Jim Collins on 'The Flywheel Effect'. https://www.jimcollins.com/concepts/the-flywheel.html

Chapter 4 Forgetting

1 Although assumptions as to the inherent moral worth of remembrance have been challenged (Connerton 2008), one of their most radical detractors is David Rieff in his *In Praise of Forgetting*. Rieff takes to task some of the canon in the field of memory studies (including Margalit, Ricoeur and Nora) who argue for the political and moral value and necessity of remembering. Rieff

(2016: 56) asks directly of memory's moral champions, 'What if they are wrong?'

2 Halbwachs 1980, p. 120.
3 Hoskins 2018.
4 Connerton 2008, p. 59.
5 Hoskins 2025b.
6 Loveday 2024.
7 Atomic-bomb survivor, interviewed by Andrew Hoskins and Luli van der Does, 2022.
8 Mrs Yoshiko Kajimoto, interviewed by Andrew Hoskins and Luli van der Does, 3 February 2022 via Zoom.
9 Jonathan Wegener, interviewed by Hoskins and Čimová via Zoom, 15 June 2021.
10 Jacobsen and Beer 2021.
11 De Figueiredo 2024.
12 Furedi 2013, 2024.
13 Hoskins 2024.
14 https://www.hereafter.ai/
15 Baudrillard 1994, p. 12.
16 See, for example, Thomsen et al. 2025.
17 Mrs Yoshiko Kajimoto, interviewed by Andrew Hoskins and Luli van der Does, 14 March 2024, Hiroshima.
18 Ibid.
19 Winter 2006, pp. 26–7. See also Ford and Hoskins 2022, pp. 121–2.
20 I am grateful to Luli van der Does for these insights.
21 Mrs Yoshiko Kajimoto, interviewed by Andrew Hoskins and Luli van der Does, 14 March 2024, Hiroshima.
22 https://research.ibm.com/blog/what-are-foundation-models
23 Slater-Robins 2025.
24 https://www.synthesia.io/post/expressive-avatars-powered-by-synthesias-new-express1-model-are-here
25 Ibid.
26 Heikkilä 2024.
27 Katz 2024a.

28 Katz 2024b.
29 Ganguly 2024.
30 Kroker 2014.
31 European Union General Data Protection Regulation (GDPR) Art. 17, Right to erasure ('right to be forgotten') https://gdpr.eu/article-17-right-to-be-forgotten/

Chapter 5 The Radicalization of Memory

1 Lowenthal 2012, p. 3.
2 Evans 2014.
3 Lowenthal 2012, p. 3.
4 See chapter 1, n. 28.
5 Young 2021.
6 https://www.foxbusiness.com/media/meta-announces-officially-end-fact-checking-across-its-us-platforms
7 Birhane, Prabhu and Kahembwe 2021.
8 Zawacki 2023.
9 Bridle 2023.
10 Leufer and Maguire 2023.
11 Hao and Seetharaman 2023.
12 Thomas 2025.
13 Booth and Milmo 2025.
14 O'Neill 2019.
15 https://model-spec.openai.com/2025-02-12.html
16 Merrin and Hoskins 2025, p. 87.
17 Weiss 2024.
18 Roose 2024.
19 Ibid.
20 Sadegi and Blachez 2025.
21 Ibid.
22 Baudrillard 1994, p. 22.
23 Runia 2014, p. 9.
24 Hsu 2025.
25 Ibid.
26 Furedi 2013, 2024.

27 Furedi 2024, p. 23.
28 Jacoby 1975.
29 Furedi 2024, p. 179.
30 Stern 2024.
31 https://www.independent.co.uk/tech/charlie-kirk-ai-images-death-b2830351.html
32 It is hard to instantly tell if the excerpts in this video are real, AI-generated, or a mix of the two.
33 https://www.france24.com/en/live-news/20250915-gaza-aid-flotilla-carrying-greta-thunberg-departs-tunisia
34 https://www.tiktok.com/@magic.ben.art/video/7549067027743362311?is_from_webapp=1&sender_device=pc&web_id=7553652467180865046
35 https://www.independent.co.uk/tech/charlie-kirk-ai-images-death-b2830351.html
36 https://www.theguardian.com/us-news/2025/sep/20/charlie-kirk-martyr-christian-nationalist-movement
37 Hannah-Jones 2025.
38 https://www.theguardian.com/us-news/2025/sep/18/what-did-jimmy-kimmel-say-said-comments-about-charlie-kirk
39 https://www.bbc.co.uk/news/articles/c701jr01dj2o
40 Donegan 2025.
41 Furedi 2024, p. 23.
42 Ibid., p. 24.
43 Bronner 2021. *Cognitive Apocalypse*, sample translation, https://www.frenchrights.com/cognitive-apocalypse
44 Ibid.
45 Boine 2023.
46 Lanier 2025.
47 Boine 2023.
48 Ibid.
49 https://www.scmp.com/news/people-culture/trending-china/article/3328737/tearful-chinese-girl-bids-farewell-broken-ai-robot-after-it-teaches-word-memory
50 Ibid.

51 https://www.theshermanlawyers.com/blog/2024/october/-is-it-considered-cheating-if-my-husband-has-a-r/
52 Cox 2024.
53 Warzel 2024.
54 Marchal et al. 2024.
55 Lanier 2025.
56 Ibid.
57 Chayka 2025.
58 Strother 2013.
59 Merrin and Hoskins 2025.

References

Barnier, A. J. and Hoskins, A. 2018. Is There Memory in the Head, in the Wild? *Memory Studies*. https://doi.org/10.1177/1750698018806440

Barnier, A. J., Sutton, J., Harris, C. B. and Wilson, R. A. 2008. A Conceptual and Empirical Framework for the Social Distribution of Cognition: The Case of Memory. *Cognitive Systems Research*. https://doi.org/10.1016/j.cogsys.2007.07.002

Baudrillard, J. 1994. *The Illusion of the End*, trans. Chris Turner. Polity Press.

Bernardi, J. 2025. Friends for Sale: The Rise and Risks of AI Companions. Ada Lovelace Institute Blog. https://www.adalovelaceinstitute.org/blog/ai-companions/

Bhabha, H. K. 1994. *The Location of Culture*. Routledge.

Bioy Casares, A. 1964. *The Invention of Morel*, trans. Ruth L. C. Simms (originally published in 1940 by Editorial Losada). New York Review of Books.

Birhane, A. 2024. Synthetic Data Is a Dangerous Teacher. *Wired*. https://www.wired.com/story/synthetic-data-is-a-dangerous-teacher/

Birhane, A., Prabhu, V. U. and Kahembwe, E, 2021. Multimodal Datasets: Misogyny, Pornography, and Malignant Stereotypes. *arXiv*. https://doi.org/10.48550/arXiv.2110.01963

Boden, D. and Hoskins, A. 1995. Time, Space and Television. Paper presented at the 2nd Theory, Culture & Society Conference, Culture and Identity: City, Nation, World, Berlin.

Boine, C. 2023. Emotional Attachment to AI Companions and European Law. *MIT Case Studies in Social and Ethical Responsibilities of Computing*. https://doi.org/10.21428/2c646de5.db67ec7f

Booth, R. and Milmo, D. 2025. Chinese AI Chatbot DeepSeek Censors Itself in Realtime, Users Report. *The Guardian*. https://www.theguardian.com/technology/2025/jan/28/chinese-ai-chatbot-deepseek-censors-itself-in-realtime-users-report

Bowker, G. C. 2007. The Past and the Internet, in J. Karaganis (ed.), *Structures of Participation in Digital Culture*. Social Science Research Council.

Bridle, J. 2023. The Stupidity of AI. *The Guardian*. https://www.theguardian.com/technology/2023/mar/16/the-stupidity-of-ai-artificial-intelligence-dall-e-chatgpt

Brock, G. 2016. *The Right to Be Forgotten: Privacy and the Media in the Digital Age*. I. B. Tauris.

Bronner, G. 2021. Cognitive Apocalypse (trans. sample from French into English of G. Bronner [2021], *Apocalypse Cognitive*). https://www.frenchrights.com/cognitive-apocalypse

Burgess, M. 2024. 'AI Girlfriends' Are a Privacy Nightmare. *Wired*. https://www.wired.com/story/ai-girlfriends-privacy-nightmare/

Caltrider, J., Rykov, M. and MacDonald, Z. 2024. Romantic AI Chatbots Don't Have Your Privacy at Heart. *Mozilla*. https://foundation.mozilla.org/en/privacynotincluded/articles/happy-valentines-day-romantic-ai-chatbots-dont-have-your-privacy-at-heart/

Cannataci, J. A. 2016. 'Report of the Special Rapporteur on the Right to Privacy', United Nations General Assembly, https://digitallibrary.un.org/record/844394?v=pdf#files

Carr, N. 2010. *The Shallows*. Atlantic Books.

Case, A. 2016. Tune in Tomorrow. *New Philosopher* 11 (February–April): 27–8.

Chan, S., Pataranutaporn, P., Suri, A., Zulfikar, W., Maes, P. and Loftus, E. F. 2024. Conversational AI Powered by Large Language Models Amplifies False Memories in Witness Interviews. *arXiv.* https://doi.org/10.48550/arXiv.2408.04681

Channell, D. F. 1991. *The Vital Machine: A Study of Technology and Organic Life.* Oxford University Press.

Chayka, K. 2025. Elon Musk's A.I.-Fuelled War on Human Agency. *The New Yorker.* https://www.newyorker.com/culture/infinite-scroll/elon-musks-ai-fuelled-war-on-human-agency

Chun, W. H. K. 2016. *Updating to Remain the Same: Habitual New Media.* MIT Press.

Clark, A. 2008. *Supersizing the Mind: Embodiment, Action, and Cognitive Extension.* Oxford University Press.

Clark, A. 2025. Extending Minds with Generative AI. *Nature Communications.* https://doi.org/10.1038/s41467-025-59906-9

Clark, A. and Chalmers, D. 1998. The Extended Mind. *Analysis.* https://www.jstor.org/stable/3328150

Clough, P. T. 2000. *Autoaffection: Unconscious Thought in the Age of Teletechnology.* University of Minnesota Press.

Connerton, P. 2008. Seven Types of Forgetting. *Memory Studies.* https://doi.org/10.1177/1750698007083889

Conway, M. A. 2005. Memory and the Self. *Journal of Memory and Language.* https://doi.org/10.1016/j.jml.2005.08.005

Cox, J. 2024. Hacked 'AI Girlfriend' Data Shows Prompts Describing Child Sexual Abuse. *404 Media.* https://www.404media.co/hacked-ai-girlfriend-data-shows-prompts-describing-child-sexual-abuse-2/

Crawford, K. 2021. *Atlas of AI: Power, Politics, and the Planetary Costs of Artificial Intelligence.* Yale University Press.

Crozatier, N. 2026. An Overview of the 'Externalization' of Memory: An Account of Technologically Extended Semantic, Episodic, and Prospective Memory. *Memory, Mind and Media.* https://doi.org/10.1017/mem.2026.10034

DaCosta, B. 2025. Speaking with the Past: Constructing AI-Generated Historical Characters for Cultural Heritage and Learning. *Heritage*. https://doi.org/10.3390/heritage8090387.

De Figueiredo, M. 2024. Our Last, Impossible Conversation. *The New York Times*. https://www.nytimes.com/2024/03/22/style/modern-love-ai-our-last-impossible-conversation.html

Dillon, M. 2007. Governing Terror: The State of Emergency in Biopolitical Emergence. *International Political Sociology*. https://doi.org/10.1111/j.1749-5687.2007.00002.x

Donegan, M. 2025. Charlie Kirk's Killing Was a Tragedy. But We Must Not Rewrite His Life. *The Guardian*. https://www.theguardian.com/commentisfree/2025/sep/14/charlie-kirk-killing

Evans, C. L. 2014. William Gibson Has No Idea How the Future Will See Us. *Vice*. https://www.vice.com/en/article/william-gibson-we-have-no-idea-what-the-future-will-think-of-us/

Fawns, T. 2022. Remembering in the Wild: Recontextualising and Reconciling Studies of Media and Memory. *Memory, Mind & Media*. https://doi.org/10.1017/mem.2022.5

Ford, M. and Hoskins, A. 2022. *Radical War: Data, Attention and Control in the Twenty-First Century*. Hurst Publishers.

Furedi, F. 2013. *Moral Crusades in an Age of Mistrust*. Palgrave Macmillan.

Furedi, F. 2024. *The War Against the Past: Why the West Must Fight for Its History*. Polity Press.

Ganguly, M. 2024. 'It's Not Me, It's Just My Face': The Models Who Found Their Likenesses Had Been Used in AI Propaganda. *The Guardian*. https://www.theguardian.com/technology/2024/oct/16/its-not-me-its-just-my-face-the-models-who-found-their-likenesses-had-been-used-in-ai-propaganda

Giddens, A. 1991. *Modernity and Identity – Self and Society in the Late Modern Age*. Polity Press.

Goode, L. 2023. Where Memory Ends and Generative AI Begins. *Wired*. https://www.wired.com/story/where-memory-ends-and-generative-ai-begins/

Groebner, V. 2007. *Who Are You? Identification, Deception and Surveillance in Early Modern Europe*, trans. Mark Kyburz and John Peck. Zone Books.

Gunkel, D. J. 2018. *Robot Rights*. MIT Press.

Halbwachs, M. 1980. *The Collective Memory*. Harper & Row.

Hannah-Jones, N. 2025. What the Public Memory of Charlie Kirk Revealed. *The New York Times Magazine*. https://www.nytimes.com/2025/09/28/magazine/charlie-kirk-rhetoric.html

Hao, K. and Seetharaman, D. 2023. Cleaning Up ChatGPT Takes Heavy Toll on Human Workers. *The Wall Street Journal*. https://www.wsj.com/articles/chatgpt-openai-content-abusive-sexually-explicit-harassment-kenya-workers-on-human-workers-cf191483

Happer, C. 2024. *The Construction of Public Opinion in a Digital Age*. Manchester University Press.

Hayles, N. K. 2006. Traumas of Code. *Critical Inquiry*. https://criticalinquiry.uchicago.edu/traumas_of_code_by_n._katherine_hayles

Heaven, W. D. 2024. Why Does AI Hallucinate? *MIT Technology Review*. https://www.technologyreview.com/2024/06/18/1093440/what-causes-ai-hallucinate-chatbots/

Heikkilä M. 2024. Synthesia's Hyperrealistic Deepfakes Will Soon Have Full Bodies. *MIT Technology Review*. https://www.technologyreview.com/2024/06/24/1094170/synthesias-hyperrealistic-deepfakes-will-soon-have-full-bodies/

Henkel, L. A. 2014. Point-and-Shoot Memories: The Influence of Taking Photos on Memory for a Museum Tour. *Psychological Science*. https://doi.org/10.1177/0956797613504438

Högberg, C. and Larsson, S. 2022. AI and Patients' Rights: Transparency and Information Flows as Situated Principles in Public Health Care, in K. de Vries and M. Dahlberg (eds), *Law, AI & Digitalization*. De Lege – Yearbook Uppsala Faculty of Law 2021. Iustus Förlag.

Hoskins, A. 2011. Media, Memory, Metaphor: Remembering and the Connective Turn. *Parallax*. https://doi.org/10.1080/13534645.2011.605573

Hoskins, A. 2015. Archive Me! Media, Memory, Uncertainty, in A. Hajek, C. Lohmeier and C. Pentzold (eds), *Memory in a Mediated World: Remembrance and Reconstruction.* Palgrave Macmillan. https://link.springer.com/chapter/10.1057/9781137470126_2

Hoskins, A. 2018. The Restless Past: An Introduction to Digital Memory and Media, in A. Hoskins (ed.), *Digital Memory Studies: Media Pasts in Transition.* Routledge.

Hoskins, A. 2024. AI and Memory. *Memory, Mind & Media.* https://doi.org/10.1017/mem.2024.16

Hoskins, A. 2025a. AI and Collective Memory. *Current Opinion in Psychology.* https://doi.org/10.1016/j.copsyc.2025.102156

Hoskins, A. 2025b. The Forgetting Ecology: Losing the Past through Digital Media and AI, in Q. Wang and A. Hoskins (eds), *The Remaking of Memory in the Age of the Internet and Social Media.* Oxford University Press. https://academic.oup.com/book/59599/chapter/503179161

Hoskins, A. and Illingworth, S. 2020. Inaccessible War: Media, Memory, Trauma and the Blueprint. *Digital War.* https://doi.org/10.1057/s42984-020-00025-8

Hoskins, A. and Illingworth, S. 2022. War as Constant Competition: The Weaponized Future and the Fantasy of Total Control, in A. Downey (ed.), *Topologies of Air.* Sternberg Press.

Hoskins, A., Čimová, K. and Pilkington, D. forthcoming. *The AI Memory Machine: Why the Past Is All Over.* Oxford University Press.

Hsu, T. 2025. The White House Frames the Past by Erasing Parts of It. *The New York Times.* https://www.nytimes.com/2025/04/05/technology/trump-history-websites.html

Hu, K. 2023. ChatGPT Sets Record for Fastest-Growing User-Base in History – Analyst Note. *Reuters,* 2 February. https://www.reuters.com/technology/chatgpt-sets-record-fastest-growing-user-base-analyst-note-2023-02-01/

Iglesias, S. et al. 2024. Digital Doppelgängers and Lifespan Extension: What Matters? *The American Journal of Bioethics.* https://doi.org/10.1080/15265161.2024.2416133

Jacobsen, B. and Beer, D. 2021. *Social Media and the Automatic Production of Memory: Classification, Ranking and the Sorting of the Past.* Bristol University Press.

Jacoby, R. 1975. *Social Amnesia: A Critique of Conformist Psychology from Adler to Laing.* Beacon Press.

Jiménez-Alonso, B. and Brescó de Luna, I. 2022. Griefbots: A New Way of Communicating with the Dead? *Integrative Psychological and Behavioral Science.* https://doi.org/10.1007/s12124-022-09679-3

Jones, M. L. 2016. *Ctrl + Z: The Right to Be Forgotten.* New York University Press.

Jurcys, P., Greenwald, A., Fenwick, M., Loikkanen, A. and Mann, S. P. 2024. Who Owns My AI Twin? Lights and Shadows of Data Ownership in a New World of Simulated Identities. *SSRN.* http://dx.doi.org/10.2139/ssrn.4940663

Katz, L. 2024a. AI Avatars Help War-Torn Ukraine Deliver Vital Services. *Forbes.* https://www.forbes.com/sites/lesliekatz/2024/09/27/ai-generated-humans-will-help-ukrainians-access-vital-services-amid-war/

Katz, L. 2024b. Ukraine Government Appoints AI-Generated Spokesperson. *Forbes.* https://www.forbes.com/sites/lesliekatz/2024/05/03/ukraine-foreign-ministry-introduces-ai-generated-spokesperson/

Kidd, J. and Nieto McAvoy, E. 2025. Synthetic Afterlives: Deathbots as Affective Infrastructures of Memory. *Memory, Mind & Media.* https://doi.org/10.1017/mem.2025.10013

Kidd, J. and Nieto McAvoy, E. (forthcoming). *AI Afterlives: Digital Memory and Synthetic Pasts.* Bloomsbury.

King, J., Klyman, K., Capstick, E., Saade, T. and Hsieh, V. 2025. User Privacy and Large Language Models: An Analysis of Frontier Developers' Privacy Policies. *arXiv.* https://arxiv.org/abs/2509.05382

Kozlovski, A. and Makhortykh, M. 2025. Digital Dybbuks and Virtual Golems: The Ethics of Digital Duplicates in Holocaust Testimony. *Memory, Mind & Media.* https://doi.org/10.1017/mem.2025.10006

Kroker, A. 2014. *Exits to the Posthuman Future*. Polity Press.

Lagerkvist, A. 2014. The Netlore of the Infinite: Death (and Beyond) in the Digital Memory Ecology. *New Review of Hypermedia and Multimedia*. https://doi.org/10.1080/13614568.2014.983563

Lambert, P. 2019. *The Rght to Be Forgotten: Interpretation and Practice*. Bloomsbury Professional.

Lanier, J. 2025. Your A.I. Lover Will Change You. *The New Yorker*. https://www.newyorker.com/culture/the-weekend-essay/your-ai-lover-will-change-you

Leong, L-Y., Teck-Soon, H., Keng-Boon, O., Wei-Han Tan, G. and Koo-Hang, A. 2025. Generative AI: Current Status and Future Directions. *Journal of Computer Information Systems*. https://doi.org/10.1080/08874417.2025.2482571

Leufer, D. and Maguire, M. 2023. What You Need to Know about Generative AI and Human Rights. *Access Now*. https://www.accessnow.org/what-you-need-to-know-about-generative-ai-and-human-rights/

Licklider, J. C. R. 1960. Man-Computer Symbiosis. *IRE Transactions on Human Factors in Electronics*. https://groups.csail.mit.edu/medg/people/psz/Licklider.html

Loveday, C. 2024. Threat from the Air: A Neuropsychologist's Perspective on Psychological and Physiological Harm. *Digital War*. https://doi.org/10.1057/s42984-023-00081-w

Lowenthal, D. 2012. The Past Made Present. *Historically Speaking* 13(4): 2–6.

Magni, F., Park, J. and Chao, M. M. 2024. Humans as Creativity Gatekeepers: Are We Biased against AI Creativity? *Journal of Business and Psychology*. https://doi.org/10.1007/s10869-023-09910-x

Makhortykh, M. 2024. Shall the Robots Remember? Conceptualising the Role of Non-Human Agents in Digital Memory Communication. *Memory, Mind & Media*. https://doi.org/10.1017/mem.2024.2

Mann, T. 2025. This Open Text-to-Speech Model Needs Just Seconds of Audio to Clone Your Voice. *The Register*. https://www.the

register.com/2025/02/16/ai_voice_clone/?mc_cid=30e3e6c233&mc_eid=39b76612ed

Marchal, N. et al. 2024. Generative AI Misuse: A Taxonomy of Tactics and Insights from Real-World Data. *arXiv*. https://doi.org/10.48550/arXiv.2406.13843

Marsh, E. J. and Rajaram, S. 2019. The Digital Expansion of the Mind: Implications of Internet Usage for Memory and Cognition. *Journal of Applied Research in Memory and Cognition*. https://doi.org/10.1016/j.jarmac.2018.11.001

Mayer-Schönberger, V. 2009. *Delete: The Virtue of Forgetting in the Digital Age*. Princeton University Press.

McDermott, K. B. and Roediger, H. L. 2014. Memory (Encoding, Storage, Retrieval). *Noba Project*. https://nobaproject.com/modules/memory-encoding-storage-retrieval

McStay, A. and Bakir, V. 2025. The Moral Threshold of AI Companionship and Desired Governance: Reflections from the UK Public. *SSRN*. http://dx.doi.org/10.2139/ssrn.5193090

Melis, R. 2019. Anonymity versus Privacy in a Control Society. *Journal of Critical Library and Information Studies*. https://doi.org/10.24242/jclis.v2i2.75

Menary, R. (ed.) 2010. *The Extended Mind*. MIT Press.

Merrill, S. et al. 2025. Handling the Hype: Demystifying Artificial Intelligence for Memory Studies. *Memory, Mind & Media*. https://doi.org/10.1017/mem.2025.10018

Merrin, W. 2014. *Media Studies 2.0*. Routledge.

Merrin, W. 2021. Hyporeality, the Society of the Selfie and Identification Politics. *Mast: The Journal of Media Art Study and Theory*. https://doi.org/10.59547/26911566.2.1.02

Merrin, W. and Hoskins, A. 2025. *Sharded Media: Trump's Rage against the Mainstream*. Palgrave Macmillan. https://link.springer.com/book/10.1007/978-3-031-84786-8

Miller, A. R. 1971. *The Assault on Privacy: Computers, Data Banks, and Dossiers*. The University of Michigan Press.

Milmo, D. 2025. Apple's UK Encryption Legal Challenge Heard behind Closed Doors. *The Guardian*. https://www.theguardian

.com/technology/2025/mar/14/apple-uk-encryption-legal-challenge-heard-behind-closed-doors

Mollick, E. 2024. *Co-Intelligence: Living and Working with AI.* W. H. Allen.

Morozov, E. 2013. *To Save Everything Click Here: Technology, Solutionism and the Urge to Fix Problems that Don't Exist.* Penguin Books.

Munir, M. 2022. Autonomous Weapons Systems: Taking the Human Out of the Loop. *SSRN.* https://ssrn.com/abstract=4074072

Murphy, G., Egan, R. and Greene, C. M. 2025. Memories for Public Events in the Internet Age: Fake News, False Memories, and Filter Bubbles, in Q. Wang and A. Hoskins (eds), *The Remaking of Memory in the Age of the Internet and Social Media.* Oxford University Press. https://doi.org/10.1093/oso/9780197661260.003.0008

Nield, D. 2023. How to Use Generative AI Tools While Still Protecting Your Privacy. *Wired,* https://www.wired.com/story/how-to-use-ai-tools-protect-privacy/

O'Flaherty, K. 2018. YouTube Keeps Deleting Evidence of Syrian Chemical Weapon Attacks. *Wired.* https://www.wired.com/story/chemical-weapons-in-syria-youtube-algorithm-delete-video/

O'Neill, P. H. 2019. How WeChat Censors Private Conversations, Automatically in Real Time. *MIT Technology Review.* https://www.technologyreview.com/2019/07/15/134178/how-wechat-censors-private-conversations-automatically-in-real-time/

Pereira, A. G., Ghezzi, A. and Vesnić-Alujević, L. (2014) Introduction: Interrogating the Right to Be Forgotten, in A. Ghezzi, A. G. Pereira and L. Vesnić-Alujević (eds), *The Ethics of Memory in a Digital Age: Interrogating the Right to be Forgotten.* Palgrave Macmillan.

Pierce, D. 2024. ChatGPT is Getting 'Memory' to Remember Who You Are and What You Like. *The Verge.* https://www.theverge.com/2024/2/13/24071106/chatgpt-memory-openai-ai-chatbot-history

Rajaram, S. 2025. Exploring Online Social Interactions in the Remaking of Memory, in Q. Wang and A. Hoskins (eds), *The Remaking of Memory in the Age of the Internet and Social Media*. Oxford University Press. https://doi.org/10.1093/oso/9780197661260.003.0012

Ratliff, E. 2025. AI Clones and the Future of Voice AI. *Big Technology Podcast*. https://podcasts.apple.com/ie/podcast/ai-clones-the-future-of-voice-ai-with-evan-ratliff/id1522960417?i=1000691384563

Reading, A. 2014. Seeing Red: A Political Economy of Digital Memory. *Media, Culture & Society*. https://doi.org/10.1177/0163443714532980

Rieff, D. 2016. *In Praise of Forgetting: Historical Memory and Its Ironies*. Yale University Press.

Risko, E. F., Kelly, M. O., Lu, X. and Pereira, A. E. 2025. Varieties of Offloading Memory: A Framework, in Q. Wang and A. Hoskins (eds), *The Remaking of Memory in the Age of the Internet and Social Media*. Oxford University Press. https://doi.org/10.1093/oso/9780197661260.003.0005

Roose, K. 2024. How Do You Change a Chatbot's Mind? *The New York Times*, https://www.nytimes.com/2024/08/30/technology/ai-chatbot-chatgpt-manipulation.html

Runia, E. 2014. *Moved by the Past: Discontinuity and Historical Mutation*. Columbia University Press.

Sadeghi, M. and Blachez, I. 2025. A Well-Funded Moscow-Based Global 'News' Network Has Infected Western Artificial Intelligence Tools Worldwide with Russian Propaganda. *NewsGuard*. https://www.newsguardrealitycheck.com/p/a-well-funded-moscow-based-global

Schacter, D. L. 2021. Media, Technology, and the Sins of Memory. *Memory, Mind & Media*. https://doi.org/10.1017/mem.2021.3

Shroff, L. 2024. Shh, ChatGPT. That's a Secret. *The Atlantic*. https://www.theatlantic.com/technology/archive/2024/10/chatbot-transcript-data-advertising/680112/

Shumailov, I., Shumaylov, Z., Zhao, Y., Gal, Y., Papernot, N. and Anderson, R. 2024. The Curse of Recursion: Training on Generated

Data Makes Models Forget. *arXiv.* https://arxiv.org/abs/2305.17493

Singer, J. A. and Salovey, P. 1993. *The Remembered Self: Emotion and Memory in Personality*. Free Press.

Slater-Robins, M. 2025. What is Synthesia? Everything We Know about the Best Enterprise AI Video Generator. *TechRadar.* https://www.techradar.com/pro/what-is-synthesia-everything-we-know-about-the-best-enterprise-ai-video-generator

Solove, D. J. and Hartzog, W. 2025. The Great Scape. The Clash between Scraping and Privacy. *California Law Review.* https://www.californialawreview.org/print/great-scrape

Stern, J. 2024. 'I Died that Day' – AI brings Back Voices of Children Killed in Shootings. *The Wall Street Journal.* https://www.wsj.com/tech/ai-brings-back-voices-of-children-killed-in-shootings-7d72cb8d

Stone, C. B. and Zwolinski, A. 2022. The Mnemonic Consequences Associated with Sharing Personal Photographs on Social Media. *Memory, Mind & Media.* https://doi.org/10.1017/mem.2022.6

Storm, B. C., Bittner, D.-L. and Yamashiro, J. K. 2025. The Changing Dynamics and Consequences of Memory Retrieval in the Age of the Internet, in Q. Wang and A. Hoskins (eds), *The Remaking of Memory in the Age of the Internet and Social Media.* Oxford University Press. https://doi.org/10.1093/oso/9780197661260.003.0006

Strother, Z. S. 2013. 'A Photograph Steals the Soul': The History of an Idea, in J. Peffer and E. Cameron (eds), *Portraiture and Photography in Africa.* Indiana University Press.

Sutton, J. 2005. Memory and the Extended Mind: Embodiment, Cognition, and Culture. *Cognitive Processing.* https://doi.org/10.1007/s10339-005-0022-x

Sutton, J. 2008. Between Individual and Collective Memory: Interaction, Coordination, Distribution. *Social Research.* http://www.jstor.org/stable/40972051

Tanner, B. 2024. Dippy AI Launches Censorship-Free, Proactive AI Companions. *Intelligent CIO.* https://www.intelligentcio.com/

north-america/2024/10/23/dippy-ai-launches-censorship-free-proactive-ai-companions/

Thomas, S. 2025. It's Not Just DeepSeek, All AI Is Censored. *The Spectator.* https://www.spectator.co.uk/article/its-not-just-deepseek-all-ai-is-censored/

Thomsen, D. K. et al. 2025. A Framework for Vicarious and Collective Memory, Future Projections and Narrative Identity. *Nature Reviews Psychology.* https://doi.org/10.1038/s44159-025-00429-x

Thrift, N. 2004. Remembering the Technological Unconscious by Foregrounding Knowledges of Position. *Environment and Planning D: Society and Space.* https://doi.org/10.1068/d321t

Wang, Q. 2022. The Triangular Self in the Social Media Era. *Memory, Mind & Media.* https://doi.org/10.1017/mem.2021.6

Warzel, C. 2024. The Slop Candidate. *The Atlantic.* https://www.theatlantic.com/technology/archive/2024/10/donald-trump-mcdonalds/680324/

Weatherbed, J. 2024. Meta Fed Its AI on Almost Everything You've Posted Publicly since 2007. *The Verge.* https://www.theverge.com/2024/9/12/24242789/meta-training-ai-models-facebook-instagram-photo-post-data

Weinrich, H. 1997. *Lethe: The Art and Critique of Forgetting,* trans. Steven Rendall. Cornell University Press.

Weiss, B. 2024. Marc Andreessen on AI, Tech, Censorship, and Dining with Trump. *The Free Press.* https://www.thefp.com/p/marc-andreessen-on-ai-tech-censorship-trump-democrats

Winter, J. 2006. *Remembering War: The Great War between Historical Memory and History in the Twentieth Century.* Yale University Press.

Xiao, T., Nerino, F. F., Matthews, H. D., Tavoni, M. and You, F. 2025. Environmental Impact and Net-Zero Pathways for Sustainable Artificial Intelligence Servers in the USA. *Nature Sustainability.* https://doi.org/10.1038/s41893-025-01681-y

Young, G. K. 2021. How Much Is Too Much? The Difficulties of Social Media Content Moderation. *Information & Communications Technology Law.* https://doi.org/10.1080/13600834.2021.1905593

Zawacki, Z. 2023. Exposing the Sexism in Generative AI. *Mozilla*. https://foundation.mozilla.org/en/blog/exposing-the-sexism-in-generative-ai/

Zittrain, J. 2024. We Need to Control AI Agents Now. *The Atlantic*. https://www.theatlantic.com/technology/archive/2024/07/ai-agents-safety-risks/678864/

Index

Page numbers in italics refer to illustrations.